THE 12 STEPS

FOR ADULT CHILDREN*

*From Addictive and Other Dysfunctional Families

THE 12 STEPS

FOR ADULT CHILDREN*

From Addictive and Other Dysfunctional Families

Friends in Recovery

RPI Publishing, Inc.
San Diego

Published by
RPI Publishing, Inc.
1201 Knoxville Street
San Diego, CA 92110-9778
(619-275-1350)

The Twelve Steps are reprinted with permission of Alcoholics
Anonymous World Services, Inc. Permission to reprint and
adapt the Twelve Steps does not mean that A.A. has reviewed
or approved the contents of this publication nor that A.A. agrees
with the views expressed herein. A.A. is a program of recovery
from alcoholism only—use of the Twelve Steps in connection
with programs and activities which are patterned after A.A.,
but which address other problems, does not imply otherwise.

ISBN 0-941405-08-7 (pbk.)

Printed in the United States of America
Second edition
15 14 13

*In memory of Edward, Cecilia and
the countless others whose lives
were a struggle with addiction,
and who never found a solution.*

*This book is especially dedicated to
those family members and friends who
have found the courage to seek recovery.*

NOTICE

This book is designed to provide information regarding the subject matter covered. It is provided with the understanding that the publisher and author are not engaged in rendering individualized professional services. These processes and questions, intended for individual or group study, are not to be a substitute for one-to-one professional therapy when such help is necessary.

NOTE FROM THE PUBLISHER

Those who participated in the writing and review of this material are recovering Adult Children from dysfunctional families. Their intention was to carry the message of the Twelve Steps to all individuals who experienced trauma in their childhood. Central to the theme of this work is that healing is possible for those individuals whose childhood has been impacted by addictive or emotionally repressive parents or guardians. The insight they brought to the writing of this book was a result of their belief that, through working the Twelve Steps and developing a loving supportive partnership with one's Higher Power, one could be restored to wholeness.

Their intention is to offer a workable tool for individuals seeking recovery. This has been achieved by presenting the conditions most commonly found in Adult Children in tandem with the Twelve Steps as adapted from Alcoholics Anonymous. The philosophical foundation for this book is based upon the Twelve Step concept that has helped millions of individuals recover from many forms of addictive, compulsive or obsessive behavior. The material emphasizes the application of one's self-understanding and awareness as a major recovery tool.

The Twelve Traditions of Alcoholics Anonymous stress personal anonymity as a vital element in one's recovery. "Friends in Recovery" have chosen to remain anonymous for that reason. We offer these materials, not as an end in themselves, but as a means to developing a healthy relationship with God and with others.

TABLE OF CONTENTS

THE TWELVE STEPS
OF ALCOHOLICS ANONYMOUS

1. We admitted we were powerless over alcohol—that our lives had become unmanageable.

2. Came to believe that a Power greater than ourselves could restore us to sanity.

3. Made a decision to turn our will and our lives over to the care of God as we understood Him.

4. Made a searching and fearless moral inventory of ourselves.

5. Admitted to God, to ourselves, and to another human being the exact nature of our wrongs.

6. Were entirely ready to have God remove all these defects of character.

7. Humbly asked Him to remove our shortcomings.

8. Made a list of all persons we had harmed, and became willing to make amends to them all.

9. Made direct amends to such people wherever possible, except when to do so would injure them or others.

10. Continued to take personal inventory and when we were wrong promptly admitted it.

11. Sought through prayer and meditation to improve our conscious contact with God as we understood Him, praying only for knowledge of His will for us and the power to carry that out.

12. Having had a spiritual awakening as the result of these steps, we tried to carry this message to alcoholics, and to practice these principles in all our affairs.

INTRODUCTION TO REVISED EDITION

This material was first written in 1986 exclusively for Adult Children who were working the Twelve Steps in a supportive environment. Since the first publication in 1987, the book has been reprinted seven times. With each printing, text changes were made which clarified and amplified the message. This revised edition reflects the spiritual and emotional growth of its contributors, who continue to work their individual programs and apply the principles of the Twelve Steps to their daily lives. They have found the root of their recovery process to be their partnership with a Higher Power. Since individual understanding of a Higher Power varies, the use of the male pronoun to describe that Power has been deleted.

The Twelve Step program enables us to share our experience, strength and hope with others. Many newcomers to the Program can relate to the Common Feelings and Behaviors but have difficulty in identifying alcoholism in their family. Many recovering professionals and individuals who are studying alcoholism and other addictions have contributed largely to the development of new insights and material relating to these issues. Their studies and experiences indicate that addictive behavior is an obsessive-compulsive disorder. It represents an obsession or craving which drives a person to compulsive use of relationships, alcohol, food, drugs, sex, gambling, etc. in order to fill an inner void or emptiness. This contribution has expanded the understanding of the term "addiction" and has been beneficial to the revision of this book.

As part of the revision of this book, the wording in Steps One, Two, Six and Seven have been altered. The changes are summarized as follows.

Step One now states that we are powerless over the effects of addiction, rather than alcohol. As research continues in the field of addiction, it is becoming evident that we are an addictive society—with addiction being so pervasive that we cannot identify all its manifestations.

Step Two has been changed to read "restored to wholeness." The philosophy of the Twelve Steps views partnership with our Higher Power as the foundation for achieving wholeness. This book is intended to help us explore our childhood family systems to discover the ways in which our wholeness was violated and our true selves gradually distorted.

Steps Six and Seven focus on working in partnership with our Higher Power in order to continue moving away from our past and toward healing and wholeness. Belief in a Higher Power does not entitle us to any magical cure or sudden relief from pain. We come to realize that the thoughts, feelings and inner urges to return to our old behaviors require our conscious effort not to repeat them again. We can gradually accomplish this task of "letting go" by asking for and depending on the love, acceptance and strength of our Higher Power. It's called Team Work.

We walked away from our dysfunctional homes and childhoods with distorted views and beliefs about ourselves and the world. Having seen ourselves reflected in our parental mirrors, we adopted beliefs that we were "not okay." In doing so, we gave up our identity and began searching for ways to feel good about ourselves. As adults, we continue this pattern by allowing others to influence our self-image, self-esteem and happiness. Our self-defeating beliefs about ourselves lead us to make self-destructive choices. Thus, we end up seeking to fill our inner emptiness with inappropriate behavior and misuse of other people, sex, chemicals, possessions, accomplishment, money, etc.

As we begin our recovery, changes in our feelings and behavior may mean we "act as if" things have changed. This "act of faith" helps us in our process toward "coming to believe" that there is a Power greater than ourselves who is there for us. This Power may be primarily a belief in our Inner Self, God, Life, etc. and only secondarily based upon an intellectual conviction. We may be comfortable thinking of our new belief as more like falling in love than adopting a philosophy.

Our journey toward wholeness is clearly one that will last for the rest of our lives. The "leap of faith" we take is not the admission that "I believe," for we can only truly believe that for which we have found sufficient evidence. It is an act of courage and risk-taking. Our first steps of faith will undoubtedly constitute looking for evidence, and the greatest evidence of all will be our firsthand experience with our Higher Power.

We take the existence and availability of the incandescent bulb for granted, but it was the faith of Thomas Edison, plus years of trial and error, that led to that discovery. Knowing that it may take us weeks, months and perhaps years to find and learn to work with our Higher Power, should we not begin? By facing the challenge presented in this book, we will be putting forth the same dedication and curiosity as Edison—sitting down before the facts as we know them, prepared to relinquish our preconceived notions.

Remembering the wisdom of the Chinese proverb about the journey of a thousand miles starting with the first step, we need only begin.

THE TWELVE STEPS AND OUR
JOURNEY TOWARD WHOLENESS

The Twelve Step program is a philosophy of life which helps us to recognize the benefits of discovering and expanding our spiritual nature. It is not a program sponsored by any particular religious group or entity. Though people using this program find it harmonious with their own personal theology and spiritual beliefs, it has no official religious affiliation. It is a program we follow at our own pace and in our own way, utilizing the help and support of our Higher Power and others who also work the Program.

This book illustrates how the Twelve Steps can be used as an initial recovery tool and later integrated into an ongoing part of our journey toward wholeness. As we begin to recognize and work on our life problems in the light of the Twelve Steps, we develop the foundation for a recovery experience that can bring about our physical, emotional, mental and spiritual well-being. An open mind and a willingness to do the work are all that is required.

The format of the Twelve Step material in this book is only one of the many creative tools available to individuals on the path toward recovery. It provides a guideline to help us achieve our goals of peace and serenity. As our relationship with a Higher Power develops, more will be disclosed to us and our lives will become less complicated. We learn to ask our Higher Power for help in understanding what we can do to take better care of ourselves. By working the Steps, greater and deeper insights will occur.

Willingness to complete this material and a commitment to work the Steps on a daily basis will provide us with the ongoing gifts of peace and serenity. As we share our experience, strength and hope we join our fellows on the journey toward wholeness and are unified in the Fellowship of the Spirit.

INTRODUCTION

As Adult Children from addictive or other dysfunctional families, we have had to face many difficulties in our lives. The attitudes, feelings and behaviors we have today are the direct result of the modeling and messages we experienced in our early environment. Because we grew up in chaos, we did not learn appropriate interpersonal or decision-making skills, or the value of recognizing cause and effect—that every behavior brings with it a consequence.

We continue to resist recognizing these limitations in ourselves. This may cause us to suffer from maladjustment and experience severe psychological, emotional and behavioral stress. Our denial is the key to that resistance. It is our defense against the reality of our condition and keeps us unaware of our compulsive or obsessive behaviors. These behaviors manifest themselves through various means, some of which are; need to be in control, lack of self-confidence or personal esteem, being victims or martyrs, an inability to express our needs and feelings and being unaware of our repressed feelings of pain, resentment, shame, fear and rage.

When a life circumstance forces us to come to terms with ourselves, we start looking for explanations. We try self-help books, therapy groups and other forms of consciousness raising. After exhausting these resources, we come to the realization that the peace we seek is not to be found in these sources. When we reach this point, we are ready to accept the support and guidance of a Higher Power. Our acceptance and reliance upon this spiritual partner is brought to fruition as we work the Twelve Steps and receive the budding miracle of our faith and efforts—the restoration of our trust, dignity, courage and newness of life.

THE TWELVE STEPS
FOR ADULT CHILDREN

STEP ONE

> We admitted we were powerless over the effects of addiction—that our lives had become unmanageable.

STEP TWO

> Came to believe that a Power greater than ourselves could restore us to wholeness.

STEP THREE

> Made a decision to turn our will and our lives over to the care of God as we understood God.

STEP FOUR

> Made a searching and fearless moral inventory of ourselves.

STEP FIVE

> Admitted to God, to ourselves, and to another human being the exact nature of our wrongs.

STEP SIX

> Were entirely ready to work in partnership with God to remove our ineffective behavior.

STEP SEVEN

> Humbly asked God to help us remove our shortcomings.

STEP EIGHT

> Made a list of all persons we had harmed and became willing to make amends to them all.

STEP NINE

Made direct amends to such people wherever possible, except when to do so would injure them or others.

STEP TEN

Continued to take personal inventory and, when we were wrong, promptly admitted it.

STEP ELEVEN

Sought through prayer and meditation to improve our conscious contact with God as we understood God, praying only for knowledge of God's will for us and for the power to carry that out.

STEP TWELVE

Having had a spiritual awakening as the result of these steps, we tried to carry this message to others, and to practice these principles in all our affairs.

To Be Honest, God

To be honest, I'm not sure who I'm praying to.
Maybe I'm talking to myself, but...

To be honest, I can't take anymore.
My life is a failure, I feel like a...

To be honest, I want to die, I want to quit,
I want to quit hurting me, I want to quit
hurting them.

To be honest, I don't know what to do.
For the first time, I'm really lost...

To be honest, I don't know if anyone hears me,
But if someone hears, please come find me.

(Taken from _12 Step Prayers for A Way Out,_ page 5-6)

Contact with our Higher Power is a vital link
to our recovery. Whether we express ourselves
through prayer or sit silently in meditation, this is
an important part of our journey. Because of this
need for communication with our Higher Power,
Friends in Recovery have produced _12 Step Prayers
for A Way Out._ This companion to _The 12 Steps—A
Way Out_ is now available. Consult your local book-
store.

COMMON FEELINGS AND BEHAVIORS
OF ADULT CHILDREN

Research involving individuals who were raised in an addictive or dysfunctional family environment has determined that certain feelings and behaviors are common in Adult Children from these homes. Although the general population demonstrates many of these behaviors, individuals from dysfunctional families tend to have a high incidence of them. This exercise is intended to help identify the areas of your life in which these feelings and behaviors are evident.

We have feelings of low self-esteem as a result of being criticized. We perpetuate these parental messages by judging ourselves and others harshly. We try to cover up our poor opinions of ourselves by being perfectionistic, controlling, contemptuous and gossipy.

We tend to isolate ourselves out of fear and to feel uneasy around other people, especially authority figures.

We are desperate for love and approval and will do anything to make people like us. Not wanting to hurt others, we remain "loyal" in situations and relationships even when evidence indicates our loyalty is undeserved.

We are intimidated by angry people and personal criticism. This causes us to feel inadequate and insecure.

We continue to attract emotionally unavailable people with addictive personalities.

We live life as victims, blaming others for our circumstances, and are attracted to other victims as friends and lovers. We confuse love with pity and tend to "love" people we can pity and rescue.

We are either super-responsible or super-irresponsible. We take responsibility for solving others' problems or expect

1

others to be responsible for solving ours. This enables us to avoid being responsible for our own lives and choices.

We feel guilty when we stand up for ourselves or act in our own best interest. We give in to others' needs and opinions instead of taking care of ourselves.

We deny, minimize or repress our feelings as a result of our traumatic childhoods. We are unaware of the impact that our inability to identify and express our feelings has had on our adult lives.

We are dependent personalities who are so terrified of rejection or abandonment that we tend to stay in situations or relationships that are harmful to us. Our fears and dependency stop us from ending unfulfilling relationships and prevent us from entering into fulfilling ones.

Denial, isolation, control, shame and inappropriate guilt are legacies from our family of origin. As a result of these symptoms, we feel hopeless and helpless.

We have difficulty with intimacy, security, trust and commitment in our relationships. Lacking clearly defined personal limits and boundaries, we become enmeshed in our partner's needs and emotions.

We tend to procrastinate and have difficulty following projects through from beginning to end.

We have a strong need to be in control. We overreact to change over which we have no control.

STEP ONE

We admitted we were powerless over the effects of addiction—that our lives had become unmanageable.

T he idea presented in Step One is overwhelming to most of us until we begin to accept the reality of our lives as they actually are. It is humiliating to admit that we are powerless and that our lives have become unmanageable. We have spent a major portion of our lives attempting to manage the behavior, thoughts and feelings of others so that we could feel safe and secure. Some of us may strive for control by appearing weak and incapable, thereby manipulating others to perform for us. We may be obsessed with achieving a superior status in life, and we find it difficult to acknowledge that we could actually be powerless. We may be preoccupied with being the smartest or the fastest, or with having the best job. Whatever we do, no matter how hard we try to make it appear okay, some of our behavior puts our health and well-being at serious risk. Step One brings us to the threshold of identifying the causes of the obsessive and compulsive behavior that we cannot control.

We realize that, in this life, we have the power to make choices about matters which affect us. In attempting to influence and manage the outcome of those choices, we may sometimes experience conflict. Prior to becoming aware of our problem, we sense that something is wrong and that life is unfulfilling in many ways. As a natural result, we desperately try to right the wrong by "fixing" things. No matter what we do or where we turn, we continue to suffer acute anxiety attacks or experience episodes of bizarre and compulsive behavior. When we finally are forced to look closely at ourselves and see that we have exhausted all other possibilities, we are ready for Step One. At this point, we have no alternative but to admit that we are powerless and that our lives have become unmanageable. For the first time, we begin to alter the course of our lives, and strive for healing.

Step One is the foundation for all the Steps. When working this Step, we begin to acknowledge the reality of our life experiences. It is important not to judge ourselves harshly—we need only to observe our behavior and admit that we are powerless to change it. As we surrender to this idea, we see our behavior, thoughts and feelings as they really are and recognize the need for greater honesty with ourselves and others. It is through confronting and admitting our powerlessness that we begin to risk being honest about our limitations.

Step One consists of two distinct parts: (1) admitting that we are powerless over the affects of addictive or dysfunctional behavior from our childhood caregivers, and (2) admitting that our lives have been, and will continue to be, unmanageable if we do not change.

Admitting our powerlessness over the affects of addictive or dysfunctional behavior from our childhood caregivers often is the catalyst that brings us to the Program.

Through the Program, we initiate a process of recovery that can transform our lives. Our ineffective behavior has not supported our well-being, and our often self-destructive lifestyle is a major factor contributing to our condition. We now understand how we obtained our distorted life-view of the world, ourselves and others. This view has been perpetuated through our acquired traits, habits and behaviors. Recalling our childhood, we realize that, years before we recognized it, we behaved ineffectively and were out of control. Even then, our obsessions were not simply habits, but, indeed, the beginning of a progressive behavioral disorder involving our mental, physical and emotional well-being.

Our minds cry out against the idea of personal powerlessness and resist acknowledging that, in reality, we are not in charge. We are accustomed to accepting full responsibility for the events in our lives, as well as in the lives of others. This supports our need to deny that we are powerless. Until we discover how we can be responsible persons and also be powerless, we cannot take the first step toward liberating ourselves from the bondage of our past. The degree to which we are able to surrender is the degree to which we acknowledge our powerlessness.

Admitting that our lives are unmanageable is as compromising to our self-image as admitting that we are powerless. We want to see ourselves as responsible adults— holding a job, managing a house and family and functioning normally. We have been taught from childhood that the only way to be successful is to be in control. We have received repeatedly the message that successful people manage their own lives, as well as the lives of others, without needing outside help.

When we accept the fact that our lives are unmanageable, we also will recognize that ultimate control of our lives is not in our hands. As we reflect on the condition of our lives, we can see that, no matter how we exerted control, the results were never quite what we planned. Realizing that our depressions and frustrations are signs that we are not as competent as we think, we become more realistic in identifying the extent of our unmanageability. We see how we rationalize our behavior by making excuses for ourselves and blaming our action or inaction on fatigue, stress or other people. As we examine our lives more objectively, including our part in what is wrong with our lives, we drop our disguises and become more honest with ourselves. We then see that our lives are clearly unmanageable and not at all what we would like them to be.

Though the first Step may seem overwhelming, it merely indicates and emphasizes our human limitations, which have been a source of discomfort to us for a long time. For most of our lives, we have tried to hide our imperfections from ourselves and others, thus avoiding the reality of our situation. Step One is the first step toward developing the humility we need to accept and rely on spiritual guidance from a Higher Power. This simple act opens the door to the healing change we seek.

In the process of accepting our powerlessness and acknowledging the unmanageability of our lives, we see that our attempts to hide our limitations have crippled us. Although working Step One can be painful, the road to recovery can only begin with honest self-confrontation and surrender. Until we do this, our progress toward recovery will be hindered. Although it is difficult for many of us to accept our present condition, we realize that we alone cannot manage our own lives or control our thinking. Admitting our human limitations forms the foundation for working each of the Twelve Steps.

STEP TWO

*Came to believe that
a power greater than
ourselves could restore
us to wholeness.*

Accepting our powerlessness leads us naturally into Step Two. By this time, we have discovered the impact that being raised in a dysfunctional family has had on our lives. Our present condition is a result of the many decisions we made to survive in that chaotic environment. We are now faced with behavior that produces unmanageable situations over which we are powerless. For some of us, belief in the strength of our self-will was all we thought we needed until, in Step One, we realized the true state of our ineffective behavior. As we accept the idea of a Power greater than ourselves, we begin to function in a healthier way, and our lives become more manageable. We recognize that we are just human beings, learning to live within our human limitations.

Step Two is referred to as the Hope Step. It is the starting point from which we begin our journey toward a more spiritual view of life. In Step One, when we recognized our condition, we felt hopeless and beaten. Step Two instills new hope, as we see that help is available if we simply take the risk to believe and trust in a Power greater than ourselves. If we follow the guidance of that Power, we no longer need to struggle. We now have a chance to dramatically decrease our old patterns of behavior and gradually become the persons we were meant to be. Step Two provides a foundation for the spiritual development that will help us achieve a greater sense of personal fulfillment.

As newcomers, we often encounter stumbling blocks when working this Step. One obstacle is the difficulty we have in believing that a Power greater than ourselves exists. Although we may be aware of many examples in which "faith as small as a mustard seed" has worked wonders in the lives of others, we may doubt that it could apply to us. If doubt persists, we could be resisting the idea of a Higher Power's healing presence. We may find it impossible to imagine that, through "believing," the intensity of our obsessions and compulsions could decrease. In time, our faith begins to grow as we recognize that even the most devout, spiritually grounded persons suffer moments of doubt.

Another problem posed by Step Two is the implication that disorder and ineffective behavior permeates our lives. Having recognized that our lives are unmanageable, we now know that we need new direction. These are powerful issues for us; they can be frightening when we face them for the first time. For many of us, they are definite contradictions of our former beliefs about ourselves and our lives.

Before entering the Program, many of us strongly resisted spiritual concepts and beliefs. We neither understood spirituality, nor felt it had anything to offer us. Our longing for the nurturing and caring parent, absent from our childhood, limited our ability to understand the concept of a trusting and loving Higher Power. Perhaps we felt that our prayers were unanswered. Our faith in a Higher Power may have been shattered by our belief that, if God exists, it is not a loving God. Often, our low self-esteem created the feeling that we were not worthy of the attention or care of a Higher Power, or that it could even exist.

In Step One, we established a foundation for accepting the existence of a Higher Power. Having admitted our powerlessness, we realize how self-will has impacted our lives. The discovery and acceptance of a Power greater than ourselves is the beginning of our turning away from our self-will. Through working the Steps, we can experience a growing trust in our Higher Power.

Many people have found that "coming to believe" is a natural result of attending meetings on a regular basis. Through working the Program, it becomes evident that something dynamic is happening. If we are willing to keep an open mind and recognize the success that others enjoy, we can expect that, in time, it will also happen for us.

When we encounter our ineffective behavior and can surrender to the Twelve Step process, the existence of a Higher Power becomes very real to us. We shift our attention from wanting to alter our behavior to understanding that life is a process of evolutionary change. This shift of focus attests to the presence of a Higher Power—assisting, empowering and enabling us to accomplish what we could not have accomplished under our own power.

During the initial stages of accepting the presence of a Higher Power, it is sometimes helpful to be consciously aware of the special occurrences around us. We can view coincidences in our lives as small miracles, gifts or simply interventions of our Higher Power. By taking the time to thank our Higher Power for simple things like "not getting a ticket for running a red light," or "receiving an unexpected call from someone we are thinking about," we learn to accept a Higher Power. Our willingness to express gratitude to this Power assists us as we "come to believe."

Step Two does not demand that we accept the definitions of God as presented by various religious organizations or specific denominations. In fact, our belief may come from simply experiencing the strength of our Higher Power's healing at work in our lives. More and more we recognize the genius of our Higher Power in the loving kindness of a friend, the loyalty of a partner, the comfort and help we receive from a person in the Program, or even the Program itself.

Belief in a Power greater than ourselves is central to becoming the happy, positive and loving persons we are truly meant to be. Our old self-centered way has possibly led us to the depths of despair and loneliness, causing us to become detached from ourselves and others. We discover that our analytical mind, with its fears, judgments, expectations and plans, cannot solve our problems. The more we try to resolve things by ourselves, or expect someone else to resolve them, the more difficult our lives become.

Step Two helps us see that our lives can be restored to wholeness. In the context of the Program, wholeness is defined as "being in sound health, not diseased or injured, not broken, damaged or defective." In this sense, we can see that aspects of our behavior are out of order. We may blame everyone and everything for our condition instead of taking responsibility for our own behavior problems. If this is our first exposure to Step work, we may be totally unaware of the extent of our condition.

Many of us have acquired certain behavior patterns and personality traits that we thought would protect us from the painful realities of life. Some of the common behavior patterns are victimization, defiance, self-centeredness and indifference. The presence of these behaviors and attitudes indicates that we suffer from some form of emotional, mental and behavioral disability.

Some characteristics of our society do not foster or encourage healthy behavior. We are taught from childhood to do what is right. Without adequate moral training, we are expected to know the difference between right and wrong, but based on our early role models, the message as to what is right and wrong was confusing and unclear. As adults, we are expected to behave responsibly and to manage our own lives competently; but in reality, we cannot do so. Frequently, our mistakes are a direct result of the distorted understanding of right and wrong that we acquired in childhood. When we can accept this, we are truly ready to admit that our behavior is ineffective in many areas.

Coming to believe in a Higher Power and admitting we behave in a destructive manner require a great deal of humility. Our previous lack of humility contributed greatly to our past ineffectiveness. As we work toward a more balanced lifestyle, we see the importance of humility in all our affairs. Our growth is considerably enhanced by our willingness to be humble and accept our humanness. As we attend meetings and work the Steps, we discover the peace and serenity possible only through surrendering our self-will and humbly seeking to improve the quality of our lives.

Greater Than Myself

Higher Power,
The sky over my head,
The generations that came before,
The stars that shine above,
The world and its creatures,
The body in which I live,
The sun that warms,
The air I breathe,
The order and way of the universe,
All these things are greater than I am.
Who am I to doubt you God?

(Taken from _12 Step Prayers for A Way Out,_ page 13-14)

STEP THREE

Made a decision to turn our will and our lives over to the care of God as we understood God.

Step Three requires that we take affirmative action as a result of the developing awareness we have gained from working the first two Steps. In Step One, we admitted we were powerless, that our lives had become unmanageable. In Step Two, we came to believe that a Power greater than ourselves could restore us to wholeness. In Step Three we make a decision to turn our lives over.

Step Three commands more of us than the first two Steps, because we are now asked to trust in a Higher Power. If we feel pressured or compromised by this request we are going too fast. Our inner child may be terrified that, if we dare trust a Higher Power and expose our behavior problems to that Power, we will be rejected. In this case, it is important to stop and take time to prepare ourselves properly. It is through these first three Steps that we set the foundation for working the entire Program and for achieving the peace and serenity we seek.

The key to effectively working Step Three lies in our willingness to turn as much of our lives as we can over to the care of God. This is difficult for many of us because we are accustomed to functioning by using self-will alone. Our mistrust may have prevented God from having a meaningful place in our lives, and the idea of letting an unrecognized Power be our guide is too unfamiliar to us. We may have learned to pray to God as we would to a celestial Santa Claus, asking for things we wanted and always expecting to receive them. We may have asked for guidance in achieving our worldly goals, but this is vastly different from turning our whole being over to a Higher Power and trusting that we will be safely guided.

If we have carefully and thoroughly worked Steps One and Two, we have accepted our behavior and are ready to turn our lives over to a new manager. We see that allowing a Higher Power to guide our lives will reduce our fears and resentments to a manageable level. We recognize how that Power's presence impacts our lives as we choose to rely on a Higher Power. We may discover how comforting it is to trust in the outcome, as we see positive changes occurring in our lives.

We can expect to experience some resistance to turning our lives over to God in the beginning. This can be attributed to our need for independence, since most of us thrive on being in charge and cling to the illusion of being free to "do our own thing." We may relinquish only the parts of our lives that are causing us the most pain. This is a start, and will build our confidence as we see that God can resolve all of our problems. We may be puzzled and confused about what is guidance and what is self-will. Our deepening partnership with a Higher Power clarifies this uncertainty as we accept the step-by-step guidance we receive.

Experience tells us that, the more patient we are with ourselves and our growth, the more positive our progress will be. Being patient enables us to more easily grasp the true meaning of recovery. If we try too hard and become obsessed with our desire to get well, our relentless urgency will block our progress, causing frustration, resentment and self-pity.

The slogan "Let Go and Let God" expresses the central theme of Step Three. The idea of "letting go" and trusting the outcome can be especially helpful when we realize that surrendering our burdens actually frees us to experience healing and growth. As long as we do the appropriate "footwork" and do not expect God to do everything, we will see that our Higher Power takes good care of us.

Our distorted thinking, formerly devoted to shoring up our fragile egos, may lead us to believe that we will be ineffective if we turn our will and our lives over to the care of God. Yet, our new experiences prove that the more willing we are to depend on a Higher Power, the more confident we become as we see the direction our lives are taking. Our growing spirituality is reflected in an inner peace—the result of accepting a Power greater than ourselves and following that Power.

Caution is an important factor in completing this Step. If we are not completely comfortable with turning our will and our lives over to the care of God, we must slow down and be more reflective. Some of us may be experiencing the intense physical and psychological impact of our ineffective behavior, begun as a way to temporarily numb emotional pain, distract our boredom or relieve our stress. Whatever our behavior involves, whether it be dependency in relationships, inappropriate use of money, drugs or food, we face the prospect of spiritual and perhaps physical death. We began this Program because the path we were taking was interfering with our effectiveness. We needed help to transform our lives and be healed. Being asked to trust in a Higher Power may present a challenge to us until we understand that it is an effective way to improve our lives.

The Twelve Steps is a spiritual program—a tool for healing. Step Three is an opportunity to let a spiritual Power greater than ourselves take charge of the rest of our lives. This liberates us from the pressure of feeling responsible for everything and everyone, or expecting someone else to take responsibility for us. As we surrender to our Higher Power and allow others to experience their own Higher Power, we develop a feeling of peace and serenity in our lives.

It is not important to fully understand how our Higher Power works in order to "let go." We need only to believe in the process to initiate our own growth and thereby enhance our well-being. If we have trouble working Step Three, it is probably because we are having difficulty with the "belief" aspect of Step Two. In this case, we need to return to Step Two before going further.

When we experience meaningful results in working Step Three, a change comes over us. We are calmer and feel that a weight has been lifted from our shoulders. It can happen suddenly or gradually, as we consciously accept the guidance resulting from our partnership with a Higher Power. If we experience a feeling of euphoria, it will not last forever—at times, we might revert to our old behavior patterns. At this point, we need only to recognize this. There are no saints in this Program—we all have "slips". However, as we work the Program daily, we become more willing and able to turn our lives over consistently.

There is a paradox in the way this Program works. The less we try to manage our own lives, the more effective we become. When we give up managing our own lives and trust in our Higher Power's plan for us, we find we are calmer and more accepting of things around us. Friends may compliment us on how well we are managing our lives. As we stop trying to restrict ourselves to a course of rigid self-discipline, people may recognize how at-ease we are in simply being ourselves.

Most of us start this Program in an effort to stop repeating painful cycles of ineffective and damaging behavior. We are usually in search of answers to the complex questions of life. In the past, some of us may have experimented with lifestyles and beliefs that appeared to offer solutions. We may have been looking for a personal relationship with a Higher Power that transcended things of this world. This life-giving experience is available through the Twelve Step Program.

STEP THREE COMMITMENT

I am now willing to enter into partnership with my Higher Power.

"Higher Power, I trust that your
guidance will free me from my ineffective behavior
so that I may better do Your will.
Free me from the personal struggles and difficulties
that are rooted in my dysfunctional family life.
Show me how to love and care for
the precious child within me.
I seek wholeness so that my life may bear witness
to those I would help of Your Power,
Your Love and Your Way of Life.
I seek to do Your Will always."

My First Prayer

I surrender to you my entire life,
    O God of my understanding.
I have made a mess of it
    trying to run it myself.
You take it, the whole thing,
    and run it for me,
According to your will and plan.

(Taken from *12 Step Prayers for A Way Out*, page 23)

STEP FOUR

Made a searching and fearless moral inventory of ourselves.

O ur entrance into the Twelve Step Program often occurs after a series of painful events resulting from reality pushing aside our fantasy world. Our resultant fears and anxieties may have weakened the defenses of our denial system and forced us to look at ourselves, acknowledging the consequences of our behavior. The shock, disbelief and acceptance of the problems in our lives form the foundation for a life-changing adventure that involves self-discovery, healing and recovery. We start by confronting ourselves and uncovering the ineffective behaviors that we developed as part of our social learning. Once we understand that we can change these thoughts, feelings and behaviors, we can then look at the ways in which we have been controlled by them. Our aim is to release their hold on us and to either let them go or, with the help of our Higher Power, transform them.

During the first three Steps, we initiated many changes that have far-reaching effects on our lives. In Step One, we admitted that we were powerless, that our lives had become unmanageable. In Step Two, we came to believe in a Higher Power as a means of restoring our wholeness. In Step Three, we made a decision to turn our will and our lives over to the care of God as we understand God.

Denial is a core component of our illness, and is found in all of us to a greater or lesser degree. It is a destructive aspect of our illness, because it keeps us locked into an increasingly deteriorating pattern of behavior. Denial consists of many complicated defenses and maneuvers that we unconsciously use to prevent ourselves from facing reality. Some recognizable forms of denial are:

- **Simple Denial:** Pretending that something does not exist when it really does (e.g., discounting physical symptoms that may indicate the presence of problems).

- **Minimizing:** Being willing to acknowledge a problem, but unwilling to see its severity (e.g., admitting to estrangement in a relationship when in fact there is overt infidelity).

- **Blaming:** Placing blame on someone else for causing the problem; the behavior is not denied, but its cause is someone else's fault (e.g., blaming your parents for your current inappropriate behavior).

- **Excusing:** Offering excuses, alibis, justifications and other explanations for our own or others' behavior (e.g., calling in sick for a partner when the actual cause of the absence is drunkenness).

- **Generalizing:** Dealing with problems on a general level, but avoiding personal and emotional awareness of the situation or conditions (e.g., sympathizing with a friend's flu symptoms when you know chemical dependency is the underlying cause of the problem).

■ **Dodging:** Changing the subject to avoid threatening topics (e.g., becoming adept at "small talk").

■ **Attacking:** Becoming angry and irritable when reference is made to the existing condition, thus avoiding the issue (e.g., being unwilling to share your feelings).

Working the Twelve Steps hels us to become aware of the denial that has protected us from facing reality. In a way, denial has helped to preserve whatever shreds of self-worth and dignity we have maintained. Step Four allows us to look at our denial system, which until now has been one of our major survival techniques. Denial also has distorted our perception and grossly impaired our judgment, rendering us self-deluded and incapable of accurate self-understanding.

An inventory is not a history. It is a list of what is occurring at the moment and does not concern the past. Looking at it this way, the task of creating a fearless inventory is easier, because we have no reason to fear the present. Writing is an especially important element of Step Four and is an essential part of the process. As we list our qualities, we discover the positive as well as the negative aspects of our traits. None of us has all of one and none of the other. It is important to keep a balanced view of our strengths and limitations. Our main goal is to accept what we discover—healing is more likely to occur if we accept ourselves exactly as we are.

As we more completely understand the origins of our behavior, we may develop an enlightened and mature perspective about being Adult Children. Much of our early trauma was caused by things over which we had no control. We can see how our wounded inner child continues to influence much of our current adult behavior. We can stop engaging in hurtful childish behavior and feeling frustrated when it appears. Step Four uncovers many childhood roots that can be transformed and healed with the help of our Higher Power. Our condition can be compared to that of a gardener who continually lops off the tops of weeds while they persistently continue to grow from the roots. This type of gardening does not complete the job, because it doesn't treat the roots that lie hidden beneath the surface. Turning our lives over to our Higher Power is vital to uprooting the memories that have affected our lives.

Resentments and fears are catalysts for our problem behaviors. They had a strong impact on the way we acted as children, and we may find them deeply influencing our adult behavior today. Resentment, among other feelings of unexpressed anger, is a source from which many mental and physical ills originate. Going through life with deep resentments can only result in feelings of victimization, discouragement and frustration, as well as poor health. If we allow our resentments to dominate us, we unknowingly give them the power to destroy us.

The destructive power of fear threatens the stability we seek in recovery. At this point in our recovery, we may find a degree of fear influencing many of our behaviors. Whatever the origin of our fear (e.g., situations of abandonment, criticism or disapproval by authority figures), it can color our thinking and control our behavior, thereby threatening our recovery. As we inventory our fears, we may notice that their presence is particularly pervasive in situations where we believe we have failed or done something wrong.

Being willing to face our resentments and fears takes courage. However, faith in our Higher Power is the taproot through which we let God come to our aid. The spiritual wasteland that results from resentments and fears can be overcome by sincerely working the Steps in partnership with the guidance of our Higher Power.

Step Four shows us how to look at ourselves and our lives honestly, possibly for the first time. If we do this carefully, a new awareness of ourselves will begin. Our increased sensitivity may help us discover some aspects of our character that are alarming or overwhelming to us. If we have carefully worked Steps One through Three, this discovery should be rewarding.

As we prepare our fourth Step inventory, we look at our character traits and review both our limitations and our strengths. Our inability to accept our limitations often produces behavior that is destructive to us and exploits the limitations of others. Our strengths are seen in behaviors that have positive effects on ourselves and others. Before we can seriously work on our problem areas, we need to acknowledge and examine our limitations. Our self-understanding will be accelerated as we discover how we talk to ourselves and others—the ideas, beliefs and attitudes that govern the ways in which we see our world and how we relate to it.

The inventory we are preparing is for our own benefit. It will be the tool for making a major breakthrough in our recovery and setting us on the road to freedom. As we write the inventory, uncomfortable and uneasy feelings may arise. If these feelings make it hard to be completely honest, denial may be at work. If this happens, we can stop for a moment for careful reflection. Reviewing the facts of our personal history will sometimes cause buried feelings to surface. The negative, unwanted and excess emotional baggage we have been carrying can be gradually put aside in light of our new understanding. As we abandon old, useless attitudes, we must remember that our Higher Power is always with us, offering the support and guidance we need to complete this work.

Light a Candle

O God of my understanding,
Light a candle within my heart,
That I may see what is therein
And remove the wreckage of the past.

(Taken from *12 Step Prayers for A Way Out,* page 33)

IMPORTANT GUIDELINES FOR
PREPARING YOUR INVENTORY

The material offered in this Step Four Inventory Guide is somewhat different from the inventory guides used in other Twelve Step Programs. Emphasis is on those feelings and behaviors most commonly found in Adult Children from homes where alcohol-related or damage-inducing behavior was prevalent. When preparing your inventory, choose the traits that specifically apply to you. Don't tackle them all at once. Use recent events and record words and actions as accurately as possible. Take your time. It's better to be thorough with some than incomplete with all.

The inventory begins with exercises on resentments and fears, followed by a series of feelings and behaviors to be examined. This process enables you to prepare yourself for Step Five. You are the primary beneficiary of your honesty and thoroughness in this inventory.

It is important to refrain from generalizing. As you will note in the example provided for "Isolation," being specific helps identify active traits. When you list specific examples, include who, when, where, what. To the best of your ability, give the names of all persons involved in the situation with you (who); record the date the behavior took place (when); indicate the place where this behavior occurred (where); and, finally, describe the feeling or behavior.

RESENTMENT EXERCISE

Our mental and physical ills are frequently a result of our being unaware of our resentments. These feelings become a part of our lifestyles when we lack faith in ourselves and our Higher Power, and feel victimized by life. Learning to deal with resentment in a healthy way is an important part of our recovery process.

Examine situations in which resentment is a problem for you. Answer the following questions when describing these conditions:

- What or whom do you resent (e.g., people, institutions, principles)?

- What causes you to feel resentful?

- How has this resentment affected the way you think, feel and behave (e.g., lowered self-esteem, diminished goals, difficulty in relationships, physical harm or threats)?

- Which character traits are active (e.g., approval seeking, control, frozen feelings)?

EXAMPLE: **I resent** my boss **because** he doesn't care to hear my explanation of why I am depressed. **This affects** my self-esteem. **This activates** my anger.

FEAR EXERCISE

Our mental and physical ills are frequently a result of our being unaware of our fears. These feelings become a part of our lifestyles when we lack faith in ourselves and our Higher Power, and feel victimized by life. Learning to deal with fear in a healthy way is an important part of our recovery process.

Examine situations in which fear is a problem for you. Answer the following questions when describing these conditions:

- What or whom do you fear (e.g., people, institutions, principles)?

- What causes you to feel fearful?

- How has this fear affected the way you think, feel and behave (e.g., lowered self-esteem, diminished goals, difficulty in relationships, physical harm or threats)?

- Which character traits are active (e.g., approval seeking, control, frozen feelings)?

EXAMPLE: **I fear** my spouse **because** I can never please him/her. **This affects** my self-esteem. **This activates** my fear of rejection.

INVENTORY GUIDELINES (LIMITATIONS)

The example below will assist you in completing your Fourth Step Inventory. Follow the suggested guidelines and be as thorough as possible. Refer to **Isolation** in the inventory section for definitions.

ISOLATION

- List specific examples of your behavior that indicate you are isolating yourself; e.g.,

  I declined an invitation to Sharon's party last Saturday.

  I did not actively participate in the management meeting.

- Identify and explain the underlying causes (fear, resentment, anger, guilt); e.g.,

  I am afraid that if I let myself go I will do something foolish. I worry about not fitting in or being conspicuous.

  I fear personal criticism if I express myself freely.

- Identify and explain what is being hurt and threatened (self-esteem, goals, security, personal or sexual relations); e.g.,

  My self-esteem is affected when I reveal myself to other people. I judge myself without mercy, and I believe they judge me. This interferes with my desire to have a love relationship and to meet new people.

  I feel my job security is at risk.

INVENTORY GUIDELINES (STRENGTHS)

The example below will assist you in completing your Fourth Step Inventory. Follow the suggested guidelines and be as thorough as possible. Refer to **Recovery from Isolation** in the inventory section for definitions.

RECOVERY FROM ISOLATION

- List specific examples of your behavior that indicate you isolate less frequently than before; e.g.,

Today I went to lunch with Diane and Evelyn. Although I felt uncomfortable and ill at ease, I was able to share in the conversation. I risked sharing some special feelings about my desire to be in an intimate relationship. I felt less threatened than in the past, because I could see that they were listening, and I trusted they would respect my confidentiality.

During last Monday's management meeting, I expressed a concern relative to increasing business expenses without sufficient increases in sales to cover the expenses. Rather than getting the criticism I expected, I was thanked for providing the insight.

- What do you hope to achieve as you become more confident about situations in which you would usually isolate yourself; e.g.,

I want to cultivate new, healthy relationships that will expand my confidence and help me be more comfortable in social settings. I hope to become more flexible so that I can learn to be spontaneous and have fun.

I want to become more assertive and participate in business settings. I believe this will give me an opportunity to realize my full potential.

REPRESSED ANGER

Anger is a major source of many problems in the lives of Adult Children. It is a feeling that we often repress, because admitting it makes us feel unsafe. In order to protect ourselves in our chaotic homes, we either denied our anger or expressed it inappropriately. Either way, it was safer to protect ourselves by simply pushing our feelings away. We were not aware, then, that repressed anger can lead to serious resentment and depression, which in turn can cause severe physical complications or stress-related illnesses. Today, denying anger or expressing it inappropriately causes problems in our relationships. We may pretend we are happy, because we feel frightened of the consequences that might arise if we express anger.

When we repress anger, we may experience:

Resentment	**Depression**
Self-pity	**Sadness**
Stress/pressure	**Lack of concentration**
Anxiety	**Physical discomfort**

RECOVERY FROM REPRESSED ANGER

Learning to express anger appropriately is a major step in our recovery. It can prompt the release of other hidden emotions and let others know our hurts and disappointments. We begin to set limits and be honest with ourselves. As we learn to express anger more appropriately, we are better able to cope with our own hostility as well as the hostility of others. Our relationships improve as we begin to feel comfortable expressing ourselves. Stress-related problems diminish, and we even feel better physically.

As we recover from repressed anger, we begin to:

Express anger appropriately	**Set limits for ourselves**
Identify hurt feelings	**Enjoy inner peace**
underlying the anger	**Reduce stress and anxiety**

APPROVAL SEEKING

As a result of our dysfunctional upbringing, we fear disapproval and criticism. As children, we desperately wanted to receive love and approval from our parents, grandparents, siblings and significant others. Because this rarely occurred for most of us, we constantly seek validation from others today. However, this need for approval seriously affects the way we pattern our lives and thinking around the needs of others. Not knowing how to love and approve of ourselves, we seek validation from others in order to feel good about ourselves, and may do things to get people to like us. This "other focus" prevents us from discovering our own wants and needs, feelings and desires. We look for reactions in others, assume what we need to do to please them, and then attempt to manage their impression of us. We strive to please everyone and often stay in relationships that are destructive to us so as not to hurt the other person.

When we have a need for approval from others, we may be:

People-pleasing	**Feeling unworthy**
Fearing criticism	**Ignoring our own needs**
Fearing failure	**Lacking self-esteem**

RECOVERY FROM APPROVAL SEEKING

As we begin to rely on our own approval and that of our Higher Power, we understand that wanting approval is okay; we learn to ask for it rather than manipulate others to get it. We accept compliments from others and learn to simply say thank you, believing that the compliment is sincere. We focus on our own desires and say "yes" when we mean "yes" and "no" when we mean "no."

As we recover from inappropriate approval seeking, we begin to:

Recognize our own needs	**Be loyal to ourselves**
Tell the truth about how	**Build trust in self**
we feel	**and others**

CARETAKING

As long as we took care of others, solved their problems and supplied their needs, we did not have time to look at ourselves. As this trait became more pronounced, we completely lost our own identity. As children, we assumed the responsibility for concerns and problems of others that were far beyond our capability to handle and, as a result, were deprived of a normal childhood. The unrealistic demands placed on us and, for some of us, the praise we received for being "little adults" made us believe we had God-like powers. Taking care of others boosted our self-esteem and made us feel indispensable. It gave purpose to our lives. As caretakers, we are most comfortable with chaotic situations in which we are often assured that we are needed. Although we often resent others for taking and not giving, we know only how to give, not receive—we are unable to allow others to care for us. We had no role models to teach us how to take care of ourselves.

As caretakers, we may:

Make ourselves indispensable	**Lose our identity**
Rescue and advise people	**Feel guilty, inadequate**
Ignore our own needs	**Become co-dependent**

RECOVERY FROM CARETAKING

As we put aside the role of caretaker, we become less and less responsible for everyone and everything, thus allowing individuals to find their own way. We give them over to the care of their Higher Power, which is the best source for their guidance, love and support. By dropping the burden of trying to meet everyone's needs, we find time to develop our own interests and lifestyles. Our obsession with caring for others is replaced by an acceptance of the fact that ultimately we cannot control the lives of others. We realize that our main responsibility in life is to our own welfare and happiness.

When we stop being caretakers, we begin to:

Stop rescuing and advising others	**Develop our own identity and interests**
Take care of ourselves	**Recognize dependent relationships**
Set limits for helping	

CONTROL

As children, we were victims. We had little or no control over our environment or the events that took place in our lives. As a result, in adulthood, we have extraordinary needs for security and predictability and end up controlling our feelings and behavior, as well as those of others. Our fears create rigidity and prevent us from being spontaneous. We trust only ourselves to complete a task or to handle a situation. We manipulate others to gain their approval and keep a tight rein of control on people and situations that allows us to feel safe. We fear that our lives will deteriorate if we give up our management position and become stressed and anxious when our authority is threatened.

Due to our need to be in control, we may:

Overreact to change	**Be judgmental and rigid**
Lack trust in others	**Be intolerant**
Fear failure	**Manipulate others**

RECOVERY FROM CONTROL

We become more aware of the way we have attempted to control people and things in order to feel safe and secure. We realize that our efforts have been useless—that others do things their own way and situations have their own outcomes, in spite of our controlling. We discover more effective ways to meet our needs when we start accepting our Higher Power as the source of our security. As we begin to surrender our wills and our lives to our Higher Power's care, we experience less stress and anxiety. We become more able to participate in activities without being primarily concerned with our own security. Saying the Serenity Prayer is helpful whenever we begin to recognize the reappearance of our need for control.

As we learn to give up control, we begin to:

Accept change	**Reduce our stress levels**
Trust in ourselves	**Find ways to have fun**
Empower others	**Accept others as they are**

FEAR OF ABANDONMENT

Fear of abandonment is an involuntary reaction to the emotional and/or physical loss of our parents that we experienced in early childhood. As children, we observed unpredictable behavior from irresponsible, emotionally unavailable adults. As their addiction increased in severity, so did their inability to parent. As children, we required more care than they were able to give us; their focus was elsewhere. As adults, we are inclined to choose partners who are also emotionally unavailable. We try to get our "love" needs met by meeting all our partner's needs in order to avoid experiencing the reality and pain of abandonment. "Pleasing," and thereby reducing the possibility of abandonment, takes precedence over dealing with relationship issues or conflicts and produces a tense environment with poor communication.

When we fear abandonment, we may:

Feel insecure	**Worry excessively**
Be people-pleasers	**Feel guilty when standing**
Avoid being alone	**up for ourselves**
Become co-dependent	

RECOVERY FROM FEAR OF ABANDONMENT

As we learn to rely more upon the ever-present guidance and love of our Higher Power, our confidence in our ability to manage our environment increases. Our fear of abandonment diminishes and is slowly replaced by the feeling that we are worthy, lovable and valuable people in our own right. We seek out healthy relationships with people who love and care for themselves. We feel more secure in revealing our feelings and talking about problems in the relationship. We exchange our old fears for trust in our Higher Power and others who show concern for us. We learn to understand and accept a nurturing and loving fellowship within our community. Our self-confidence grows as we begin to realize that, with a Higher Power in our lives, we will never again be totally alone.

As fear of abandonment diminishes, we begin to:

Be honest about our feelings	**Consider our own needs in**
Feel comfortable being alone	**a relationship**
Express confidence	**Talk about relationship**
	problems

FEAR OF AUTHORITY FIGURES

Fear of people in roles of authority can be a result of our parents' unrealistic expectations of us—wanting us to be more than we were able to be. Their judgmental, critical, blaming style and their inconsistent anger have had an influence on how we interact with others. We see people in authority as having unrealistic expectations of us and fear we cannot meet their expectations. Simple assertiveness displayed by others is often misinterpreted by us as anger or an attempt to control us. This can cause us to feel intimidated, and we may react in our oversensitive and fragile way. In order to avoid confrontation or criticism, we compromise our integrity and values to accommodate those of the person in power. Unable to appreciate how competent we are, we compare ourselves to others and conclude that we are inadequate.

Fear of authority figures may cause us to:

Fear rejection and criticism	**Compare ourselves to**
Take things personally	**others**
Become arrogant to cover	**Insist on being right**
up	**Feel inadequate or**
	incompetent

RECOVERY FROM FEAR OF AUTHORITY FIGURES

As we begin to feel comfortable with people in roles of authority, we learn to put criticism in a more positive light and discover that it can be a tool for learning. We recognize people in authority as being like us, with their own fears, defenses and insecurities. When we stop taking things personally, we will realize how their behavior does not determine how we feel about ourselves. We start evaluating situations and choosing our behavior rather than merely reacting to others. We recognize that our ultimate authority figure is a Higher Power who is always with us.

As we become comfortable with authority figures, we begin to:

Act with increased	**Accept constructive**
self-esteem	**criticism**
Stand up for ourselves	**Interact easily with**
	people in authority

35

FROZEN FEELINGS

Many of us have difficulty admitting that we have feelings, much less expressing them. As children, our feelings were met with disapproval, anger and rejection. As a means of survival, we learned to hide our feelings or repress them entirely. As adults, we carry stored feelings of pain, guilt, shame and rage deep within us, often unaware of their existence or intensity. We can only allow ourselves to have "acceptable" feelings in order to feel "safe." The way we respond to life and living is distorted in order to protect ourselves from the reality of what we are actually feeling. Distorted and repressed feelings cause resentment, anger and depression, which can, in time, lead to physical illness.

When we have frozen feelings, we may:

Be unaware of our feelings	**Experience depression**
Have distorted feelings	**Develop physical illness**
Repress our feelings	**Have shallow relationships**

RECOVERY FROM FROZEN FEELINGS

As we get in touch with our feelings and learn to express them, exciting things may begin to happen. Our stress levels decrease as we learn to express our feelings honestly. We learn that expressing our true feelings is a healthy way to communicate and, as a result, we may find others sharing their feelings with us. As we begin to release our stored feelings, we will undoubtedly experience some pain. But as our willingness to allow our feelings to surface increases, the pain lessens, and we find ourselves less frightened and overwhelmed by them. The more willimg we are to risk releasing our emotions, the more capable we will become of having effective and intimate relationships with ourselves, our Higher Power and others.

As we experience and express our feelings, we begin to:

Identify our feelings	**Experience our true self**
Openly express feelings	**Express our needs to**
Increase intimacy levels	**others**

ISOLATION

We find it safe in many instances to withdraw from surroundings that are uncomfortable for us. By isolating ourselves, we prevent others from seeing us as we really are. We tell ourselves that we are not worthy and, therefore, do not deserve love, attention or acceptance. We also tell ourselves that we cannot be punished or hurt if we don't express our feelings. Rather than take risks, we choose to hide, thereby eliminating the need to face an uncertain outcome.

When we isolate ourselves, we may be:

Fearing rejection	**Feeling defeated**
Experiencing loneliness	**Self-pitying**
Judging ourselves	**Seeing ourselves as different from others**

RECOVERY FROM ISOLATION

As we begin to feel better about ourselves, we become more willing to take risks and expose ourselves to new people and surroundings. We seek friends and relationships that are more nurturing, safe and supportive than our past relationships. We learn how to participate and enjoy group activities. It becomes easier to express our feelings when we recognize that people will accept us for who we really are. In turn, our self-acceptance and growing self-esteem allow us to experience the precious gift of living more comfortably and serenely.

As we isolate less often, we begin to:

Accept ourselves and others	**Be less self-centered**
Cultivate supportive relationships	**Actively participate with others**
Express our emotions	

LOW SELF-ESTEEM

During childhood, we were never encouraged to believe in our own abilities. As a result of constant criticism, we believed we were "bad" and the cause of our family problems. To feel loved and accepted, we tried harder to please, to be perfect and above reproach. The harder we tried, the more frustrated we became; no matter what we did, we could never please the "big people." We held ourselves in low esteem, affecting our ability to set and achieve our goals. Fearful of making mistakes, we avoid taking risks. We feel responsible for things that go wrong and don't accept credit when something goes right. Instead, we feel undeserving and wait for the "other shoe to drop."

When we experience low self-esteem, we may:

Be non-assertive	**Isolate from others**
Fear failure	**Have a negative self-image**
Appear incompetent	**Need to be perfect**
Fear rejection	

RECOVERY FROM LOW SELF-ESTEEM

As we work with our Higher Power to see ourselves and our abilities more realistically, our self-esteem increases. We are able to interact with others more confidently and to accept ourselves as we really are, valuing our strengths as well as our limitations. We become more willing to take risks. Recognizing that we can learn from our mistakes, we find we can achieve things we never dreamed possible. We feel safer as we come to know others and allow them to know us. Relationships become healthier, because we are able to trust and validate ourselves and no longer need to look to others for validation.

As our self-esteem increases, we begin to:

Be more confident	**Love and care for ourselves**
Act more assertively	**Openly express feelings**
Interact more easily with others	**Take risks**

OVERDEVELOPED SENSE OF RESPONSIBILITY

As children in a dysfunctional home, we felt responsible for being or creating our parents' problems. We tried to be "model children" and make the problems go away. We believed that we were responsible for the way our parents felt and behaved, even for the outcome of events. Today, we remain super-sensitive to the feelings and needs of others and assume responsibility for creating their feelings and meeting their needs. It is important to us to do our job perfectly. We volunteer to do things so others' lives will be easier and less stressful. This exaggerated sense of responsibility causes us to take on far more than we can handle effectively. We often end up feeling victimized, abused, unappreciated and resentful.

When we are overly responsible, we may:

Take life too seriously   **Be high achievers**
Be inflexible   **Have false pride**
Be perfectionists   **Manipulate others**
**Assume responsibility for
others**

RECOVERY FROM OVERDEVELOPED
SENSE OF RESPONSIBILITY

Accepting the fact that we are not responsible for the actions and feelings of others forces us to focus on ourselves. We understand that we do not control the lives of others and that people are responsible for themselves. As we assume responsibility for our own thoughts, feelings and actions, we become aware that our Higher Power, not our over-responsible nature, is our source of guidance. In this way, we learn to make the time and find the energy to support and nurture ourselves first, then give appropriately to others.

As we stop being overly responsible, we begin to:

Take care of ourselves   **Accept our limitations**
Enjoy work and leisure time   **Delegate responsibility**

39

REPRESSED SEXUALITY

We find ourselves confused and uncertain about our sexual feelings toward others, particularly those to whom we are close or those with whom we hope to be emotionally intimate. We have been trained to think of our sexual feelings as unnatural or abnormal. Because we do not share our feelings with others, we have no opportunity to develop a healthy attitude about our own sexuality. As small children, we may have explored our physical sexuality with peers and been severely punished. The message was "sex is dirty, is not talked about and is to be avoided." We may have been molested by a parent or close relative who was out of control. As a result, we are uncomfortable in our sexual roles. We do not freely discuss sex with our partners for fear of being misunderstood and abandoned. We may confuse love with sex and give our bodies indiscriminantly or agree to sex when we really just want a hug. As parents, we may avoid discussing sexuality with our children, thus denying their need for guidance and modeling in the development of their own sexual identities.

Due to repressed sexuality, we may:

Feel guilt and shame	**Use sex to feel good**
Lose our sense of morality	**about ourselves**
Be confused about our	**Experience frigidity or impotency**
sexual identities	**Manipulate others by**
Be lustful	**seductive behavior**

RECOVERY FROM REPRESSED SEXUALITY

As we increase our self-love and our ability to take care of ourselves, we begin to appreciate our bodies and our sexual desires as normal and natural. As we seek out other healthy people who love and take care of themselves, we learn to express and ask for affection appropriately. We are less fearful of commitment and better prepared to enter into a healthy relationship—emotionally, intellectually and sexually. We feel more secure in sharing our feelings, desires and limits. Our self-confidence grows and allows us to be vulnerable. We give up the need for perfection in ourselves and others and, in so doing, open ourselves to growth and change. We are honest about our own sexuality with our children. We accept their need for information, as well as their need for healthy sexual identities.

When we accept our sexuality, we begin to:

Communicate appropriately	**Consider our own sexual**
about our sexual needs	**needs**
Share intimate feelings	**Accept our sexual selves**

STEP FIVE

Admitted to God, to ourselves, and to another human being the exact nature of our wrongs.

When working Step Four, we concentrated on exposing and examining the reality of our lives. If we were honest and thorough, taking inventory was not easy. It took great courage to venture into uncharted waters and face the facts we discovered about ourselves. Step Four usually exposes unresolved feelings, unhealed memories and personality flaws that have caused resentment, depression and loss of self-worth. Following the process carefully enabled us to confront the denial and self-deception that have been "normal" patterns of action and interaction in our lives.

Thoroughness in the fourth step has helped us to confront the reality of our behavior and the impact it has had on our lives. If we were able to uncover some of the situations that formed our complex behavior patterns, Step Five can be most effective and rewarding. Achieving a balance in the inventory by focusing equally on our limitations and strengths has served to increase our self-awareness and, hopefully, our self-esteem. It has presented us with an opportunity to accept the various aspects of our character. For those who have been honest and thorough, the writing in Step Four has been a gratifying experience, preparing us for Step Five and the many new discoveries to come.

It is important to recognize that our relationship with our Higher Power provides the foundation for developing the courage and strength we need to accomplish the healing we seek. Relying on our Higher Power can help us become more willing to take risks, thus making it possible for us to proceed to Step Five. An effective fifth Step is possible only if we are satisfied with our work in Step Four. By making a searching and fearless moral inventory, we are better prepared to face reality and complete the requirements of Step Five.

Step Five provides a pathway out of our isolation and loneliness. It is a step toward wholeness, happiness and a real sense of renewal. It tests our humility, in the sense that we see ourselves as we really are—one of many human beings, all children of God. As we develop humility, we will feel more secure and self-accepting when admitting to God the exact nature of our wrongs.

In Step Five, we admit the exact nature of our wrongs to God, to ourselves and to another human being. It is important to share as much as we possibly can, as the degree to which we cleanse ourselves determines the degree to which we will be ready to proceed with our lives. As our guilt and pain is relieved, we will feel as though a great weight has been lifted from us.

Before proceeding, refer to Guidelines for Preparing Your Fifth Step (page 45).

Step Five provides an opportunity to say things out loud. It may be our first attempt at speaking the truth about ourselves as we now understand it. This can serve to assist us as a future positive communication skill. In completing the fifth Step, our final meeting with another person will first be "rehearsed" by admitting our wrongs to God and ourselves. It can be a rewarding experience.

We begin Step Five by admitting our wrongs to God. This brings us closer to ultimately surrendering to a Higher Power—"Letting Go and Letting God." To attain this goal, we must give up our need to control things and offer ourselves, our desired outcomes and our lives to our compassionate Higher Power. Admitting our wrongs to God is not for God's benefit. It is an opportunity for us to know that our Higher Power loves us and is patiently waiting for us to admit to and learn from our ineffective behavior. In doing this we experience an inner acceptance of our Higher Power and others.

Admitting to ourselves the exact nature of our wrongs is the least threatening part of Step Five and can be done with minimal risk. It does not test our honesty or expose our self-deception. Talking only to ourselves prevents us from having to place ourselves in a realistic perspective. Deceiving ourselves is a well-cultivated talent. In the past, we have manipulated our own thoughts and feelings so that we saw only what we wanted to see. However, the admission of our wrongs to ourselves is an important first step in preparing us for our conversation with another human being.

Nothing draws us to each other like honesty and humility. These qualities illustrate our humanity and are truly attractive to others. If we have been humble and honest with God and with ourselves, completing the final stage of Step Five will be relatively easy. Success in this part of Step

Five depends on our finding the right person with whom to share ourselves—one with whom we feel comfortable and trusting.

The most difficult part of Step Five is admitting our wrongs to another human being. Allowing another person to see parts of us that have been hidden even from ourselves can be a frightening experience. We may be concerned that we will be laughed at or rejected. This Step seriously challenges our ability to be completely honest and willing to accept the consequences.

When selecting the person in whom we will confide, we need to look for a dependable person who is familiar with the Program. Trusting the person we choose is essential to feeling safe when we describe ourselves and our behavior. Our ability to share honestly and intimately will be enhanced if we accept our limitations as humans, realizing that none of us is perfect.

When preparing to expose our innermost selves to another person, we need to do more than just talk—we need to be ready, and willing, to listen. If we are willing to listen with an open mind to someone else's viewpoint, we will broaden our awareness and provide ourselves with an opportunity to change and grow. The two-way nature of this encounter is vital to us as a part of our process of self-revelation. Questions and comments shared in a caring and understanding manner often reveal feelings and insights of which we were unaware. We are sometimes amazed to find that other people have experienced painful histories much like our own.

We need to be realistic and understand that our long-standing behaviors have become habits that may be extremely difficult to break. Admitting the exact nature of our wrongs does not ensure that they won't be repeated. While we do not plan to have lapses, it is natural to presume that they will occur. Maintaining close contact with our Higher Power will help us to face and deal with them as they happen.

As we complete Step Five, we begin to experience the reality of God's love for us through the way in which our feelings about ourselves are changing. Knowing that our Higher Power is with us helps us make a critical advancement toward healing—that of accepting our humanness.

IMPORTANT GUIDELINES FOR PREPARING YOUR FIFTH STEP

Choose your Fifth Step listener carefully—one who is familiar with Twelve Step Programs. The individual can be:

- a clergyman ordained by an established religion; ministers of many faiths often receive such requests.

- a trusted friend (preferably of the same sex), a doctor or psychologist.

- a family member with whom you can openly share. Be careful not to disclose information that might be harmful to spouses or other family members.

- a member of a Twelve-Step Program. If you are working with family groups as described in this book, you may find trust already exists and will deepen by doing your Fifth Step with a group member. In some cases, the family group as a whole can be the listener.

In preparing for the Fifth Step, either as communicator or listener, the following suggestions are helpful:

- Begin with prayer, asking your Higher Power to be present as you prepare to go through your Fourth Step revelations and insights. Ask God to guide and support you in what you are about to experience.

- Allow ample time to complete each thought and stay focused on the subject. Discourage unnecessary explanations.

- Eliminate distractions. Telephone calls, children, visitors and extraneous noises should be eliminated.

- Remember that Step Five asks only that we admit the exact nature of our wrongs. It is not necessary to discuss how the wrongs came about or how changes will be made. You are not seeking counsel or advice.

- As the listener, be patient and accepting. You are your Higher Power's spokesperson and are communicating unconditional acceptance.

- As the listener you are there to help the communicator express thoughts clearly. Ask questions when necessary so the information can be clearly understood by both of you.

- When Step Five is completed, both parties can share their feelings about the experience. It is now possible to extend to each other the love our Higher Power extends to us individually.

- Observe confidentiality. What you have shared is personal. Nothing defeats honesty and damages relationships faster than a betrayed confidence.

The following information is helpful when completing your Fifth Step with God:

- Step Five is for your own benefit—your Higher Power already knows you. You are beginning a process of living a life of humility, honesty and courage. The result is freedom, happiness and serenity.

- Imagine your Higher Power sitting across from you in a chair.

- Start with a prayer: e.g., "Higher Power, I understand that you already know me completely. I am now ready to openly and humbly reveal myself to you—my hurtful behaviors, self-centeredness and traits. I am grateful to you for the gifts and abilities that have brought me to this point in my life. Take away my fear of being known and rejected. I place myself and my life in your care and keeping."

- Speak out loud, sincerely and honestly sharing your understanding of the insights you gained from your Fourth Step inventory. Be aware that emotions may surface as part of the powerful cleansing experience taking place.

- The objective is balance. Remember that each of your character traits has a strength and a limitation. Begin with resentments and fears, then proceed to those traits you have included in your Fourth Step Inventory.

The following information is helpful when completing your Fifth Step with yourself:

- Writing your Fourth Step inventory began the process of developing your self-awareness, the first step toward what will become genuine self-love. Solitary self-appraisal is the beginning of your admission, but it is insufficient in itself. The Fifth Step is where you turn that knowledge into enhanced self-acceptance.

- Sit in a chair facing an empty chair that serves as your imaginary double. Or sit in front of a mirror that allows you to see yourself as you speak.

- Speak out loud. Allow yourself time to hear what you are saying and to note any deeper understanding that occurs.

- Acknowledge your courage for proceeding to this point. This and every part of this process releases ex-

47

cess emotional baggage that you have carried around because of low self-worth.

The following information is helpful when completing your Fifth Step with another person:

- Simply stated, it takes considerable humility to bare ourselves to another person. We are about to reveal our self-defeating, damaging and harmful character traits. We will also disclose our positive and contributing traits. We must do this to remove the stage-characters mask we present to the world. It is a bold step toward eliminating our need for pretense and hiding.

- Review the guidelines for choosing your Fifth Step listener when selecting a person to assist you in completing your Fifth Step. Begin your sharing with the **Resentment** and **Fear Exercises** in your workbook and then proceed by analyzing the character traits you wrote about.

You may never see that person again, which is okay. It is your decision to continue the relationship in whatever direction you choose, from casual friendship to deeper spiritual companionship.

After completing your Fifth Step, take time for prayer and meditation to reflect on what you have done. Thank your Higher Power for the tools you have been given to improve your life. Spend time rereading the first five Steps and note anything you have omitted. Acknowledge that you are laying a new foundation for your life. The cornerstone is your relationship with your Higher Power and your commitment to honesty and humility.

Congratulate yourself for having the courage to risk self-disclosure, and thank your Higher Power for the peace of mind you have achieved.

STEP SIX

Were entirely ready to work in partnership with God to remove our ineffective behavior.

Our willingness to work Steps One through Five indicates our readiness to complete Step Six. Steps One and Two prepared us for Step Three, at which time we made a decision to turn our will and our lives over to the care of God as we understood God. Steps Four and Five helped us uncover our behavior flaws, facing them courageously and sharing them with God, ourselves and another human being. We have acknowledged our shortcomings and confronted our guilt. Guilt feelings are natural, but clinging to them will halt our progress. We have learned that blaming and punishing ourselves seriously inhibits our growth.

Step Six is another opportunity to relinquish our self-will. The partnership and trust we have developed in our Higher Power is the benchmark of our readiness to have our ineffective behavior removed. Most of us have seen healing take place in our lives and the lives of others. Our work to this point has been directed toward cleansing our wounds. We now prepare ourselves to let go and let God help us do the healing that is necessary.

Our current ineffective behavior stems from many of the traits we have identified. We probably acquired many of these behaviors in childhood, and as adults we continue to use them as a means to survive the chaos and imbalance in our lives. As we become more aware of these behaviors and accept them without fault-finding, we can better deal with them from a position of choice. With the help of our Higher Power, we can use our decision-making ability to perform and express ourselves in a more positive way. Our Higher Power always allows us the freedom to decide how we will deal with our damaging behavior. By being honest with ourselves and our Higher Power, and trusting that we will experience healing, we develop a foundation of strength and hope to draw upon as we meet life's challenges.

In our culture, self-will is a highly valued trait. Some of us learned at an early age that we must always strive to improve ourselves. Our parents, teachers and employers emphasized our responsibility to overcome our limitations. As a result, when we accumulate rewards and demonstrate success, we are acknowledged and applauded as being "self-made." It is a rare person who attributes individual success to following the will of a Higher Power.

It is natural for us to be comfortable with many of our behaviors. Because they have become familiar tools to us, the thought of having them removed can be threatening to our security. As difficult as it may seem, we must be willing to let go of the ineffective behaviors to become "entirely ready" to have God assist us in removing them. Being "entirely ready" requires a dedication much like preparing for a race, learning to speak in front of an audience or developing artistic skills—it requires a lot of practice.

Preparing to be "entirely ready" to have God help us remove our character flaws is accomplished through systematic repetition of the training we have undergone in the first Five Steps. We have experienced confidence in the ongoing process of working and living the Steps one day at a time. Being "entirely ready" requires faith and belief that our Higher Power knows what we need. As we become willing to relinquish our own self-will and to trust that only the harmful behaviors will be removed, we learn about the gifts God has for us.

The task of removing our ineffective behavior is more than we can handle alone. Step Six does not indicate that we are the ones to do the removing; all we have to do is be "entirely ready" for it to happen. It is a state of being, not something that we actually do. We reach this state of being by faithfully working the Program, whether or not we feel like we are making progress. When we are "entirely ready," our reservations about letting God assist us in removing our shortcomings will have lessened.

With some of the more deeply rooted disabling behaviors, we may find it necessary to move into the role of a "detached observer." By becoming an observer of our behavior and the behavior of others, we can become more aware of how we act or react in various situations. When we see ourselves thinking negatively, or doing something destructive, we can make a note of it and ask for help from our Higher Power. By distancing ourselves as an observer, the task of realizing the depth of our ineffectiveness will become much easier.

Some people reach a state of preparedness quickly and are ready early in their recovery to help God remove their harmful character traits. However, for most of us the process is a gradual one. Our insecurities may cause us to cling to old habits and unproductive ways of thinking. This blocks the process of change and the flow of inspiration. When this happens, one way to become receptive to God's help with this blockage is to turn to our Higher Power through prayer and meditation.

It is beneficial to analyze the ways in which we communicate with God. Thinking about the way in which we phrase our statements will illustrate the distinction between asking and admitting. *"Dear God, I want to be more patient"* is making a demand and telling God what we want. *"Dear God, I need help with my impatience"* is simply acknowledging the truth about ourselves. This allows God to make the best decision about how to guide us.

As we live the principles of the Program in our daily lives, we gradually and often unconsciously become ready to have our ineffective behaviors removed. Our first insight is that we are somehow different—we have changed. The change is often noticed by others before we become aware of it. The approval-seeking person begins to function more appropriately; the control addict becomes warmer and more relaxed; the super-responsible individual is no longer victimizing himself by doing for others what they can do for themselves. People who work the Program as an integral part of their lives become calmer and wear genuinely happy smiles. Much of the change we achieve by working the Program is accomplished without our conscious awareness.

A radiant, confident personality exists in each of us, hidden under a shroud of confusion, uncertainty and pain. If someone were to ask us, in our present state of recovery, whether or not we want to be free of our destructive behaviors, we would have only one answer—we are "entirely ready" to help God remove them.

STEP SEVEN

*Humbly asked God
to help us remove
our shortcomings.*

Attaining greater humility is the foundation of the Twelve Step Program. Through acceptance of ourselves, our strengths and our limitations, we develop the desire to seek and do God's will. Working and living Steps One and Two required a degree of humility so that we would admit our powerlessness and come to believe that a Power greater than ourselves could restore us to wholeness. In Step Three, humility allowed us to turn our will and our lives over to the care of God as we understood God. Without humility, Steps Four and Five would have been extremely difficult. In Step Six, our degree of readiness to have our ineffective behaviors removed was directly proportionate to our degree of humility.

The emphasis in Step Seven is on our ability to develop and practice humility. This occurs as we develop conscious contact with our Higher Power and regularly seek guidance in the affairs of our lives. Shifting our focus enables us to have our needs met in a healthy non-codependent way. This shift produces harmony with our Higher Power and other people. As we grow in the Program, we begin to understand that humility is a necessary ingredient for our healing. Only by a deepening understanding of this requirement can we adequately prepare to ask God's help in removing our shortcomings.

We seek humility because we realize it is the only way to achieve peace, serenity, happiness and manageability in our lives. Our desire to be a maturing, growing, useful and joyous person requires an inner calm, even in a turbulent, unbalanced world. Learning to accept things we cannot change, and to ask God for the courage to change the things we can, will help us achieve these desires.

Humbly asking God to help remove our shortcomings does not necessarily mean that they will all disappear at one time. They are usually shed one by one, so it is important to deal with them individually, preferably with the easiest ones first, so that we build confidence in our progress. Our commitment to working the Program one day at a time supports the idea that with God's help, progress will come at a comfortable pace. If we ask God to remove an ineffective behavior and it is not immediately removed, becoming discouraged or angry is inappropriate. We need to be patient and realize that we have more work to do. We may not be entirely ready to release the particular defect we are focusing on, or we may not have humbly asked God for help.

Positive preparation for removing our shortcomings demonstrates our willingness to let go of our destructive behaviors and cooperate with our Higher Power in the healing process. We cannot expect our circumstances to change if we continue to behave in ways that are hurtful to ourselves and others, while simply waiting for God to do all the work. Even though we have turned it over to God and have asked for help, we should be aware of our tendency to repeat old behaviors. If we do become aware of "old behaviors" at work, we can simply observe them and not be overly judgmental with ourselves. God loves us the way we are, and the realization that we are repeating destructive behavior patterns is an opportunity for us to forgive ourselves as God forgives us.

When reflecting on the recurrence of behaviors that we consider destructive or "immature," it is wise to remind ourselves that our inner-child has not matured. With our love and parenting, the wounded child within us can evolve spiritually, mentally, emotionally and behaviorally. Any improvement, however small, is cause for gratitude and joy. Remember that this process of spiritual development is designed to last a lifetime, yet we practice it one day at a time—or one minute at a time when necessary.

No matter how hard we try, we can never hope to eliminate all the negative thoughts or ineffective behaviors from our lives. In spite of all the praying we do for guidance, we may sometimes react inappropriately and cause pain to ourselves and others. Achieving sainthood is not a part of this Program. We simply do the best we can, understanding and accepting our humanness without catering to it. Our intentions may be good, but they do not protect us from occasional lapses. We need only to acknowledge our limitations and humbly ask God for help in removing our shortcomings.

Letting go of old negative behavior patterns, however destructive they may be, can create a sense of loss and require time to grieve. It is normal to grieve the loss of something we no longer have. If, in our childhood, people or "things" were taken from us before we were ready to release them, we may be overly sensitive and thereby resist experiencing the feelings that accompany the loss of familiar behaviors. Rather than using our own ineffective strategies to avoid or deny our fears, we can turn to our Higher Power for help and support. Even though our childhood learning did not adequately prepare us to handle the grieving for adult losses, our love and trust in God can heal our memories, repair the damage and restore us to wholeness.

Approaching Step Seven, we realize that we have entered into a natural "partnership" with our Higher Power—with healing and wholeness as its primary aim. In this partnership, we cannot take credit for the actual removal of our ineffective behavior. We can credit ourselves with the "footwork" necessary for that removal and our Higher Power with the support and guidance we receive. Changes will occur, but perhaps not how we expected, or in our desired time frame. God assists us in removing our character flaws when we are ready. When we humbly ask God to do the removing, we are not responsible for the outcome, but we are responsible for the preparation—for being "entirely ready."

The items remaining in our inventory after completing this process are there for a reason. We have an opportunity to accept these remaining negative behaviors and allow God to transform them into positive traits. This can be a rewarding and exciting experience. Leaders may be left with a quest for power but with no desire to misuse it. Lovers may be left with exquisite sensuality but with enough sensitivity to refrain from hurting those they love. The materially wealthy may continue to be, but will set aside their greed and possessiveness.

Practicing the Steps on a daily basis until they become routine will help us reach our goals of peace, serenity, happiness and manageability. By doing so, we will eventually be capable of breaking the hold that our old habits and behaviors have had on our lives. We will begin to trust the thoughts and feelings we have that are a result of our conscious contact with God. We will learn that the guidance we receive from our Higher Power is always available; all we need to do is listen and act in spite of our fear.

Serenity Prayer

God, grant me
The serenity to accept the things I cannot change;
The courage to change the things I can; and
The wisdom to know the difference,
Living one day at a time;
Enjoying one moment at a time;
Accepting hardship as the pathway to peace;
Taking, as you did, this sinful world as it is,
not as I would have it;
Trusting that you will make all things right
if I surrender to your will;
That I may be reasonably happy in this life,
and supremely happy with you forever in the next.

(Taken from *12 Step Prayers for A Way Out*, page 107)

SERENITY PRAYER EXERCISE

The following examples are intended to help you in using the Serenity Prayer as part of your ongoing recovery process. It is a tool that can be used daily when seeking God's help.

God, grant me the serenity to accept the things I cannot change . . . .

I can't make _____ like me and praise me.

the courage to change the things I can . . . .

I can change the way I think and feel about myself.

and the wisdom to know the difference . . . .

between the satisfaction of giving myself love and approval and the temporary satisfaction of depending on __ for it.

God, grant me the serenity to accept the things I cannot change . . . .

the way I was victimized as a child.

the courage to change the things I can . . . .

my current feelings about being victimized.

and the wisdom to know the difference . . . .

between having to do something to survive and being able to choose how I feel and act.

STEP EIGHT

Made a list of all persons we had harmed, and became willing to make amends to them all.

Step Eight brings us to the end of isolation from from ourselves, our community and our Higher Power, and sets the course for restoring our relationships. We release the need to blame others for our misfortune and accept responsibility for our own lives. Our Step Four inventory revealed how our behavior caused injury to us as well as to others. In Step Eight, we document our personal conflicts with others, citing the dates and listing the names of all the people involved. We cannot effectively change our behavior until we look at our past and eventually make restitution where needed. This is accomplished through careful examination and thoughtful analysis of what happened, when and to whom.

The first seven Steps are personal, in that they focus on examining our past behavior patterns and making us aware of our personal strengths and limitations. Step Eight begins the process of making adjustments to our lives as a result of what we have discovered in the previous Steps. By the time we reach this point in recovery, we realize how important it is for us to let go of the painful memories of our past and the circumstances surrounding them. Releasing the past opens the door to healing and to a new life for us, a life based on living one day at a time in harmony with ourselves and others.

To find fulfillment in recovery, we first learn to identify our feelings of guilt, shame, resentment and low self-worth, as well as fear of situations and other people. Once we identify these feelings, we then ask our Higher Power for help in removing them. This may seem like an awesome task, because we probably have been controlled by these negative feelings for as long as we can remember. Now, for the first time, we have an opportunity to experience a sense of personal integrity and self-authority by working the Steps. We can put our faith and trust in this process, because it has worked miracles for millions of people.

The first part of Step Eight specifically states that we list those persons whom we have harmed. When making the list, many of us may encounter a wall of resistance. It can be a severe shock to realize that we must make face-to-face admissions of our past wrongs to those with whom we have had conflict. It was humiliating enough to admit our wrongs to ourselves, to God and to another human being in Step Five. In Step Nine, we will actually make direct contact with the people concerned.

If we have conscientiously worked the first five Steps, we are usually aware of the harm we have caused to others by the time we reach Step Eight. We may even see that we have become our own worst enemies, by allowing our attitudes toward ourselves to create excessive self-blame, guilt and shame. Guilt is remorse over having done or not done something we believe to be important. It is often an appropriate response to the regret we feel for actions or inactions that conflict with our personal values. Shame is a feeling of being deeply flawed or defective as a person, and causes us to view ourselves as bad or worthless. These are all unhealthy views of ourselves that can lead us into severe depression.

We start Step Eight by making a list of the people with whom we feel uncomfortable. We make the list without being concerned about the details; simply making the list enables us to follow where our mind takes us. The list may include family members, business associates, friends, creditors, neighbors. Its length is not important, yet the list may reveal a somewhat unrealistic view of what we believe to be the power of our own personal influence. Step Eight prepares us for the ongoing process of healing that this Program offers. Our willingness to risk honesty enables the healing to take place.

Step Eight asks that we face the truth of our behavior and become willing to make amends. We also should be prepared to willingly accept the consequences and take whatever measures are necessary to make restitution. This means fully and completely acknowledging our part in the circumstances where someone was harmed as a result of our action or inaction. Accepting responsibility and making appropriate restitution are vitally important activities. Only through expressing genuine regret for our behavior can we complete the housecleaning necessary for putting the past behind us and achieving the peace and serenity we desire.

Willingness is the next key element in completing Step Eight. Being willing to forgive ourselves, as well as those who have caused us harm, is an important aspect of this process. This may require a great deal of humility from us. We are already aware that having resentments and holding grudges are luxuries we cannot afford—they not only destroy our serenity and well being but they are more harmful to us than to the persons we resent. Harboring a resentment or grudge is like having an open wound eating away at us. It causes discomfort and makes us angry, bitter and ill-tempered. These feelings can deplete our energy, making us very difficult to be around.

In the past, we were engrossed in our problems and incapable of examining our interaction with others. We became resentful, blaming and revengeful. An effective means of overcoming our resentments and hurtful feelings is recognizing that we are not always victims of circumstances—we have a responsibility for what happens in our lives. Accepting this level of responsibility demonstrates that we have reached a new level of compassion and understanding toward ourselves and others. It shows our willingness to actively pursue the possibility of change and improvement in our behavior. Through acceptance, forgiveness and turning to our Higher Power for guidance, we can let go of our need to hang onto feelings about old issues that may never be resolved.

Step Eight helps us identify the damage we have done and prepares us for Step Nine. Our continued growth requires that we make amends, in order to reduce the likelihood of repeating our unhealthy patterns of behavior. A forgiving attitude will assist us with this work. If we do not accept and forgive ourselves, we cannot accept and forgive others. If we do not accept and forgive others as they are, we cannot make amends with dignity, self-respect and humility. Making amends without extending forgiveness is meaningless and can lead us into further arguments or disputes. Our capacity to make amends must stem from a sincere desire to forgive and be forgiven.

When looking at those we have harmed, we see that our ineffective behavior played a major part in sabotaging our lives and our relationships. For example:

- When we became angry, we often harmed ourselves more than others. This may have resulted in feelings of depression or self-pity.

- Persistent financial problems resulting from our irresponsible actions caused difficulty with our family and our creditors.

- When confronted with an issue about which we felt guilty, we lashed out at the other person rather than look honestly at ourselves.

- Frustrated by our lack of control, we behaved aggressively and intimidated those around us.

- Because of our indiscriminate sexual behavior, true intimacy was impossible to achieve or maintain.

- Our fear of abandonment sometimes destroyed our relationships, because we did not allow others to be themselves. We created dependency and tried to control their behavior in an effort to maintain the relationship as we wanted it to be.

Practicing humility will help us see that other human beings have an equal right to live the life of their choice. This does not mean we have to agree with everyone about everything, but that we can choose to stop resenting, hating and wishing harm to people because their views are different from ours. Our own sanity will be preserved, and our serenity greatly enhanced, if we can forgive and extend goodwill to those who disagree with us.

As we proceed through the Steps, we can indeed learn to forgive, like and even love those whose values differ from ours. In doing so, we will understand the conflicted and oppositional part of ourselves. If we are willing to make amends and face our past, we will become more tolerant and forgiving, less rigid and judgmental. As this happens, we gradually realize that our Higher Power is doing for us what we could never do for ourselves. As our viewpoints, attitudes and beliefs change, we can participate in the process of reconciliation and move on to Step Nine, actually making the amends that are necessary.

It's About Me

Help me remember, God, that this program is about me. I find myself wanting to judge and blame and accuse everyone but myself. I'm supposed to be making a list of all those I have harmed, yet my mind is full of those who have offended me. Is this some sort of mental defense mechanism to keep myself from facing the pain I've caused others?

Help me get over this stumbling block. I release those who hurt me. I forgive. I put those people in your hands, God. Vengeance is yours. Wait God...don't punish them. I'm just as guilty...don't punish me.

Help me make things right.

(Taken from *12 Step Prayers for A Way Out,* page 61)

AMENDS LIST GUIDELINES

The following are three main categories in which we may have caused harm and for which we may want to make amends.

Material Errors: Actions which affected an individual in a tangible way, such as:

- Borrowing or spending extravagance; stinginess; spending in an attempt to buy friendship or love; withholding money in order to gratify yourself.

- Entering into agreements that are legally enforceable, then refusing to abide by the terms or simply cheating.

- Injuring or damaging persons or property as a result of our actions.

Moral Errors: Inappropriate behavior in moral or ethical actions and conduct, including questions of rightness, fairness or equity. The principal issue is involving others in our wrongdoing:

- Setting a bad example for children, friends or anyone who looks to us for guidance.

- Being preoccupied with selfish pursuits and using other people in the process.

- Inflicting moral harm (e.g., sexual infidelity, broken promises, verbal abuse, lack of trust, lying).

Spiritual Errors: "Acts of omission" as a result of neglecting our obligations to God, to ourselves, to family and to community.

- Making no effort to fulfill our obligations and showing no gratitude toward others who have helped us.

- Avoiding self-development (e.g., health, education, recreation, creativity).

65

- Being inattentive to others in our lives by showing a lack of encouragement to them.
- Forgetting birthdays, holidays and other special occasions.

AMENDS LIST

Person	Relationship	My Errors	Effect on Others	Effect on Me
Joan	wife	angry insults	fear, anger	guilt, shame
John	co-worker	sexual advances at party	distrust, shame	loss of self-respect

STEP NINE

*Made direct amends
to such people wherever
possible, except when to
do so would injure them
or others.*

S tep Nine is another action step and requires that
we confront issues from our past that may have
been dormant for a long time. This Step clearly requires
courage, as well as a renewed dedication to freeing ourselves from the guilt we feel about inflicting injuries upon
others. The extraordinary life-restoring benefits we will receive greatly compensate for the risk of making amends.

The painful memories, which still may be fresh in our
minds, can encumber us. They seriously affect our vitality
and impair our joy for living. Making amends can divest
these memories of their power and ability to affect our present thoughts, feelings and behaviors. Making amends to
a person with whom we have had an uncomfortable experience can be compared to the release of a butterfly trapped
in the hands of a curious child. Letting go gives both parties the opportunity to explore and move about indepen-

dently and naturally; a new relationship now exists between them. Each person can redefine their own role and move toward greater interdependence and comfort in the relationship.

Clear judgment, courage and determination are qualities we need when taking Step Nine. It is wise to reflect carefully upon the amends we intend to make. Our objective is not to gain peace of mind at the expense of causing grief to others, but to obtain it in a way that is beneficial for all parties. Forethought and sensitivity will help us decide on an appropriate time, place and form in which to make our amends. It will also help us find ways to keep from causing further harm. We also may choose to seek guidance from a trusted friend, and ask our Higher Power for support in this process.

Step Nine requires that direct amends be made wherever possible. We may procrastinate by telling ourselves the time is not yet right. We may be tempted to skip the more humiliating and dreaded meetings, or to make excuses to avoid the meetings. We may delay because we are afraid; it is a fearful step we are about to take. Our fear is normal and natural, as we are facing an unknown outcome. We can turn the outcome over to our Higher Power, trusting that we will benefit from whatever happens. We also can rely on the courage of our Higher Power, when we have none. Accepting the consequences of our past behavior and taking responsibility for the impact we have had on others are the core and essence of Step Nine.

Amends will be possible with almost everyone, even those who may not be aware of the harm done, since we can inflict harm by thoughts and words as well as by actions. If someone is unable to accept our apology and restitution, their part of the problem will have to remain unresolved. Our only responsibility is to make sincere amends. In these instances, the Serenity Prayer will help to restore and preserve our peace of mind.

When preparing to make amends, we see that there are various categories into which amends fall. They are:

People who are readily accessible and can be approached as soon as we are ready.

These include family members, creditors, co-workers and others to whom we owe an amend, and may involve friends as well as enemies. It is harder to approach an enemy than a friend, but we may find it more beneficial. When we are ready to face the consequences of our shared past, we will be able to go to anyone, admit the damage we have done and make restitution. The generous response of most people to such sincerity may astonish us. Not infrequently, our severest and most determined critics will meet us more than halfway on our first attempt.

Situations that will not allow us to make direct personal contact.

These refer to those who are no longer accessible, are deceased, or might be further harmed by our amend (e.g., someone already in poor emotional or physical health). In these cases, indirect amends can satisfy our need for reconciliation. We can make indirect amends through prayer or by writing an unmailed letter, as if we are actually communicating with the absent person. Indirect amends to family members can be made by sharing our amend with, or doing a special kindness for, someone else's child or parent, when we no longer have the opportunity to do it for our relative. We can make important amends to our adult children by respecting their adulthood and maintaining our own recovery as healthy adults, both physically and emotionally.

People to whom we can make only partial restitution because complete disclosure could cause harm to them or others.

These people may include spouses, ex-partners, former business associates or friends. We must analyze the potential harm to them should complete disclosure be made. This is especially true in cases of infidelity or promiscuous behavior. Amends in this area can cause irreparable damage to all parties involved. Even in cases where the matter can be discussed openly, we should be extremely careful to avoid harming third parties. Making the burdens of others harder to bear does not lessen our burden. Amends for unfaithfulness can be made indirectly by changing behavior or by concentrating sincere affection and attention on the one who has been deceived.

In cases involving serious consequences, such as potential loss of employment, imprisonment or alienation from one's family, we need to weigh the consequences carefully. We should not be deterred from making amends by fear of incurring injury to ourselves or causing injury to others. If we delay our amends merely out of fear for ourselves or others, we will ultimately be the ones to suffer. In these situations, we can seek outside guidance from a counselor or close friend to determine how to proceed. Otherwise, we will delay our growth, as well as experience stagnation in our progress toward building a new and healthier life.

Situations which require deferred action.

Seeking another opinion could be helpful, when we have assessed that a particular amend might best be deferred. It is seldom wise to approach an individual who continues to suffer from our injustices. In situations where our own hurts are still deeply felt, waiting to make amends also might be wise. We know that amends must be made eventually, but timing is important so that we can benefit from the experience and not cause additional pain to ourselves or others.

The process of making amends should not be confused with making apologies. When we apologize, we express regret for a fault or offense. An apology does not require action or imply a change in behavior. When we make an amend, we take action to improve, correct or alter that which we believe needs to be corrected. Apologies are sometimes appropriate, but apologies are not amends. We may discover, in apologizing, that we are using excessive explanation to excuse our behavior rather than simply change. We can apologize a hundred times for being late for work, but this will not "mend" our former tardiness. Appearing on time is a change in behavior, and thus becomes an amend.

Occasional emotional or spiritual relapses, or "slips," are to be expected and need to be dealt with in a compassionate and timely manner. When relapses occur, they are signals that we are probably hungry, angry, lonely or tired and are not being as vigilant as we might otherwise be. We may have even reclaimed control of our will from our Higher Power and need to go back to Step Three; or have eliminated something from our inventory and must return to Step Four; or have a character trait that we are not yet ready to relinquish and should repeat Step Six.

In reality, the Twelve Steps are intended to be repeated as we move toward our goal. Most of us need to repeat all or part of the Steps regularly, depending on our specific needs at a particular time throughout our course of recovery. After the first or second time through, we may not need to repeat the Steps in order. As we grow spiritually, we will be increasingly able to use them daily, as we journey toward further healing and a new life.

By repairing the damage we have done to others, we also will be overhauling our own lives. If we are thorough with our amends, we will find ourselves blessed with an amazingly peaceful state of mind, free of guilt and resentment. We may feel satisfaction in knowing that we have honestly done everything in our power to satisfy every material, moral and spiritual debt we have incurred—intentionally or unintentionally.

The importance of Step Nine to our recovery process is obvious—it gives us a chance to put aside prior distractions and obsessions from our past, and to start living in the present. Since we have created and used this opportunity to repair past wrongs, we can now feel good about ourselves for our efforts to replace misery with serenity. The relief or joy we may give to others will never exceed the peace and increased self-esteem and acceptance this Step brings to us.

AMENDS GUIDELINES

The following is a summary of ideas and procedures that have been useful in preparing for and making the amends required in Step Nine.

Attitude

- Being willing to love and forgive yourself and the person to whom an amend is to be made.
- Knowing what you want to say and being careful not to blame the person with whom you are communicating.
- Taking responsibility for your part in the incident, what you are going to say and how you are going to say it.
- Being willing to accept the consequences.
- Resisting the desire for a specific response from the other person.
- Being willing to turn your anxieties over to God.

Preparation

- Devoting time to prayer and meditation.
- Delaying the amend if you are angry or upset and doing more Step Four inventory work.
- Keeping it simple. Details and explanations aren't necessary.
- Remembering that the amend does not focus on the other person's part in the situation.
- Expressing your desire or asking permission to make the amend. For example: *I am involved in a program that requires me to be aware of the harm I have done to others and to take responsibility for my actions. I'd like to make amends to you. Are you willing to receive them?*

Sample Amends

- *I was (scared, overwhelmed, feeling abandoned, etc.) when _____ happened between us. I ask your forgiveness for (harm done) and for anything else I may have done in the past by my thoughts, words or actions that caused you pain. It was not my intent to hurt you. Will you forgive me?*
- *I want to make an amend to you about _____ . For all those words that were said out of (fear, thoughtlessness, etc.) and confusion, I ask your forgiveness.*

Ninth Step Prayer

Higher Power,
    I pray for the right attitude to make my amends, being ever mindful not to harm others in the process. I ask for your guidance in making indirect amends. Most important, I will continue to make amends by staying abstinent, helping others, and growing in spiritual progress.

(Taken from *12 Step Prayers for A Way Out*, page 66-67)

STEP TEN

Continued to take personal inventory and, when we were wrong, promptly admitted it.

O ur initial work with the Steps identifies the true nature of the ineffective and unhealthy behavior we have been using for most of our lives. We have examined our condition and made restitution for our misdeeds wherever possible. For many of us, the Steps may be our first antidote for relieving the pain created by our addictive behavior. Our commitment to continue working the Steps acknowledges our intention to improve the quality of our lives and relationships through reliance on our Higher Power.

Step Ten initiates the maintenance phase of the Program. As it becomes apparent that spiritual growth is a lifelong process, we then understand that our progress must be maintained daily. When we accept the fact that healing can be achieved only one day at a time, the urgency to "finish the Program" diminishes.

As we begin to feel better about ourselves and our lives, some of us may think we are "home free" and allow other activities to distract us or keep us from attending and participating in meetings. We may rationalize that we are too tired or have more important things to do. Some of us may even justify dropping out completely, in the belief that we are "cured." We may become irritable and short-tempered, not realizing that our recovery has been seriously jeopardized. If we continue on this course of self-deception, we may ultimately regress to an even greater degree of ineffectiveness.

We should be alert to the danger signals (e.g. irritability, frustration, anxiety) that occur if we slip away from the philosophy of the Steps. New problems and confusions may be related to not fully accepting the Program, missing meetings, or losing our support system. If and when we decide to return to the meetings, we may find ourselves quickly revived by the warmth and enthusiasm that surrounds us. The emotional and spiritual uplift that meetings often inspire can encourage us to get back on the path with renewed effort. When the Twelve Step philosophy of life becomes an integral part of our daily activities, our attendance at meetings may decrease. Although we may not need to attend meetings regularly, we can be assured that they are there when we need them.

Step Ten requires that we continue to take personal inventory and, when wrong, promptly admit it. This is a critical part of our recovery—we can no longer risk indulging in harmful attitudes and inappropriate behaviors. We must watch for signals that reactivate past resentments and fears or that suggest we are trying to manage our lives alone. When we see ineffective behaviors returning, we must stop ourselves and ask our Higher Power for help in removing them, then make amends promptly if harm has been done.

Our commitment to completing the remaining Steps requires that we fully acknowledge our need for continued and ongoing spiritual development. Just as our bodies tell us when to eat or sleep, our spiritual nature tells us when we need nourishment. We recognize that diligence in taking care of ourselves spiritually, emotionally and physically is necessary. As we begin to appreciate the idea that we are whole and complete, we are able to see the long-range possibilities for our future security. With the help of our Higher Power, we slowly become more able to "Let Go and Let God." As we learn to do this, our stress level greatly diminishes. The routine practice of Step Ten maintains our honesty and humility, and helps us to maintain our progress in recovery.

The Program's emphasis on daily inventory is based on the realization that many of us haven't yet developed the tools necessary for self-appraisal. As we become more familiar and comfortable with personal inventories, we become more willing to invest the necessary time in exchange for the rewards received. Three types of inventories are recommended; each serves a different purpose. These are the **Spot-Check Inventory, Daily Inventory** and **Long-Term Periodic Inventory.**

Spot-Check Inventory

This is a brief review of our thoughts, feelings and actions, done several times a day, as needed. It is a tool for examining each situation, seeing where we are wrong and taking prompt corrective action. Taking frequent inventories and promptly admitting our wrongs keeps us free from guilt and supports our spiritual growth.

In our daily activities, it is often hard to recognize that seemingly praiseworthy actions are, in fact, old behavior returning. For example, we may have a desire to do a favor for someone, and, in the process, we observe how considerate we are—how no one else would do what we are doing. Close examination of this behavior may indicate that we are still seeking approval and attempting to please others.

Another tendency is to blame someone else for our wrong-doing. We may become righteously indignant and lose our tempers. We then try to justify our anger rather than take personal responsibility for our behavior. If we are sincerely working the Program, we will realize that our anger was not related to the other person's actions at all—it was a result of our own fears, anxieties and feelings of insecurity.

Daily Inventory

A review of the day's activities serves different and complementary purposes. It reminds us that this Program is lived one day at a time. It keeps us focused on today and prevents us from worrying about the future or living in the past. This inventory is much the same as our Step Four inventory, except we are concerned only with today. The review is brief and can be done just before going to sleep.

Situations may arise that challenge our integrity and commitment. In these cases, we need to be as honest and clear about our intentions as possible. Things to consider are:

- If we are slipping back, trying to control and manipulate others, we need to recognize it, take steps to correct it, then ask our Higher Power for help and guidance.

- If we are comparing ourselves to others and feeling inferior, we need to reach out to supportive friends and examine our feelings, in order to renew our own sense of self-acceptance.

- If we are becoming obsessive or compulsive and not taking care of ourselves, we need to stop and ask our Higher Power for help, not only in determining the unmet needs we are trying to fulfill, but also how to meet these needs.

- If we are fearing authority figures, we need to find the reason for our fear, acknowledge it, and ask our Higher Power for help in reacting appropriately.

- If we are depressed, we need to discover the central issue that is causing us to feel withdrawn or sorry for ourselves.

- If we are withholding our feelings, becoming uncommunicative or giving in to others' wants and needs, we need to take the necessary risks and express our feelings assertively.

Long-Term Periodic Inventory

This is done once or twice a year and gives us a chance to reflect on our progress from a long-term perspective. Through this inventory, we will be able to see and celebrate the remarkable changes we have made in our lives. This is a time for humility and gratitude—a time to remember that our progress results from the spiritual growth we have attained through our partnership with our Higher Power. Long-term inventories also help us recognize problem areas and make necessary corrections. We may uncover previously undiscovered ineffective behavior as a result of our careful analysis.

Taking regular inventories proves invaluable as a means of keeping in touch with where we are and how we are behaving. It helps us determine if we are "on course" or slipping back into old behavior patterns. Being gentle and loving to ourselves and to our inner-child is a compassionate journey, made with a sincere desire to be restored to wholeness. Our Program is an individual one; it is reflected in how well we use the tools of the Program, namely the Twelve Steps. Our Higher Power is compassionate—watching lovingly as we falter and guiding us back on our feet when we ask for help. When an old behavior reappears or a new one is identified, we may want to keep the following points in mind:

- When old behaviors reappear, they are simply repetitions of learned patterns of behavior. They reflect choices of our unconscious mind as it defended us against feelings of pain, strife, helplessness, guilt, revenge, disapproval, etc. Clinging to these patterns keeps us from achieving the spiritual growth we so desire.

- We feel safe when something is familiar to us, even though it is a negative behavior pattern or addiction from the past that may ultimately cause us pain. We use it anyway, because it is familiar to us.

- We victimize ourselves by allowing the past to occupy our thoughts. We can let go of the past by acknowledging the unmet responsibilities that created our struggle.

- Releasing an old behavior pattern can be frightening. By surrendering it to our Higher Power, we learn to trust that we will receive the needed support to develop behaviors that are more appropriate for our present wants and needs.

- We can reach out to loving and supportive friends. They are important ingredients in our recovery.

The ongoing practice of Step Ten has many benefits; most importantly, it strengthens and maintains our recovery. We find additional rewards in many areas, such as:

- Relationship problems diminish. Taking inventory and admitting our wrongs promptly dissolves many misunderstandings without further incident.

- We learn to express ourselves, rather than fear being "found out." We see that, by being honest, we do not need to hide behind a false front.

- We no longer have to pretend we are flawless and, thus, can be candid about admitting our wrongs.

- Through admitting our own wrongs, others may, in turn, become aware of the ineffectiveness of their own behavior. We develop a true understanding of others and become capable of intimacy.

To effectively work Step Ten, we need to pay special attention to promptly admitting our wrongs. Delay in admitting them merely shows us how deeply ingrained some of our behavior patterns are. The sooner we are able to admit our wrongs, the sooner we can repair the harm done to ourselves and others. Vigilance in taking a daily inventory will help us develop a feeling of freedom, as we learn to promptly take care of things that bother us. Having taken an honest, in-depth look at ourselves, we are now ready to explore our relationship with our Higher Power and the community in Steps Eleven and Twelve.

Tenth Step Prayer

I pray I may continue:
To grow in understanding and effectiveness;
To take daily spot-check inventories of myself;
To correct mistakes when I make them;
To take responsibility for my actions;
To be ever aware of my negative and self-defeating
attitudes and behaviors;
To keep my willfulness in check;
To always remember I need your help;
To keep love and tolerance of others as my code; and
To continue in daily prayer how I can best serve
    you, my Higher Power.

(Taken from *12 Step Prayers for A Way Out*, page 75)

STEP ELEVEN

Sought through prayer and meditation to improve our conscious contact with God as we understood God, praying only for knowledge of God's will for us and for the power to carry that out.

S tep Eleven is a means to deepen our partnership with our Higher Power. Having developed a relationship in Steps Two and Three, we have relied upon it heavily as we worked the subsequent Steps. In many cases, it was the single source of courage and strength for achieving our level of progress in the Program.

At this point, we may have noticed that *"making a decision to turn our will and our lives over to the care of God"* is not a single event; it is a daily intention. Now we are being asked to *"pray for knowledge of God's will for us and for the power to carry that out."* We may find that seeking knowledge of God's will for us is an easier task than turning our will over, because of our previous persistent and repeated feelings of distrust in a Higher Power.

If we are periodically puzzled by the daily temptations and challenges we face, it may be because we are still Adult

Children, learning to distinguish between "adult" and "childlike." Most of us are continually learning how to re-parent our fear-filled inner child. In his book "Your Inner Child of the Past," Dr. Missildine addresses our need to be aware of adult behavior that stems from damaging childhood experiences (e.g. temper tantrums, perfectionism, compulsive drinking or eating, careless spending and selfishness). We clearly are not doing God's will when we insist on living in a fantasy, ignoring our failures and pressing on in ever-widening circles of confusion.

Our intention to do God's will can, at times, be compromised by the appearance of our old feelings and controlling attitudes. As we experience this struggle on a daily basis, the need for help from our Higher Power becomes more clear. In Step Eleven, we focus on deepening our relationship with our Higher Power. It is mostly through our quiet moments of prayer and meditation that the presence and guidance of a Higher Power becomes clear to us. As our relationship with our Higher Power improves, we see how we can rely and depend upon that Power for courage and strength in meeting life's challenges. We may experience a spiritual awakening that comes when we are willing and able to acknowledge, from the depth of our being, that a Higher Power can and will direct our lives.

Step Eleven requires that we improve our conscious contact with God, as we understand God. To do this, we need to be consistent, patient and willing to practice. We have made contact with God in three of the earlier Steps. In Step Three, we made a decision to turn our will and our lives over to God's care. In Step Five, we admitted our wrongs directly to God. In Step Seven, we humbly asked God to help us remove our shortcomings. Step Eleven gives us a means of strengthening that contact and enables us to bring our Higher Power into our daily lives. Now we can let go of our feelings of aloneness and alienation and enjoy the quality partnership that is truly life-giving and life-sustaining.

The means suggested for improving our conscious contact with our Higher Power are prayer and meditation. These are two of the channels through which we reach God—and experience God's reach toward us. Prayer can mean focused thought, a talk directly with God or a request for guidance and knowledge of God's will in our affairs. Meditation is listening to God. Meditation techniques are designed to calm our minds and rid us of daily preoccupations and concerns, so we can hear God's guidance and will for our lives.

How do we pray, and for what do we pray? Many of us were taught to pray before we understood what it meant. In the beginning, we may have used the prayer *"Now I lay me down to sleep,..."* or asked God to bless Mommy and Daddy and others who were close to us. As we grew, our dysfunctional family experiences brought us great pain; those we depended upon hurt and disappointed us. Perhaps we blamed God for not hearing and answering our desperate prayers. Based on the Program's principles, our attitudes toward prayer change as we work the Steps. We learn to ask that God's will for our lives be shown to us, trusting that our best interests will be served. The old habit of praying for material things will diminish, to be replaced with prayers for guidance. We begin to rely upon some of the slogans and prayers, such as "Let Go and Let God" or The Serenity Prayer. Our prayers can be simple sentence prayers, such as *"God, please help me,"* or *"Thank you, Higher Power."* God will hear and respond to our most humble call for aid.

Meditation is an ancient practice that involves the use of specific processes for calming the mind. During meditation, we establish a channel through which we can receive guidance from God. To meditate, we must quiet our conscious mind and remove the barriers established by our busy thoughts. This is difficult for some of us, because we are unaccustomed to sitting still and relaxing both body and mind. Meditation helps to calm us emotionally, relax us physically and release the unproductive energy we normally expend to keep our emotions and bodies in high gear.

Methods of prayer and meditation may vary; however, it is our desire to hear and feel heard that matters. Our primary commitment is to deepen our relationship and expand our communication with our Higher Power. This means being honest about our feelings and thoughts, admitting our limitations and bringing our failings to God for forgiveness. Through a faithful and disciplined dedication to prayer and meditation, we become aware of God's unconditional love, forgiveness and constant presence in our lives. If we continue to pray with patience and trust, we will be rewarded with endless gifts of peace, serenity, love and joy.

In our quest toward a spiritual awakening, Step Eleven provides us with a way to improve our conscious contact with God. In this Step, we pray *"only for knowledge of God's will for us and for the power to carry that out."* Great benefits can be derived from this Step when we are able to ask for knowledge of God's will, then turn the outcome over to God. It takes courage to let go of the outcome and have patience to wait for the results.

The miracle of this Step is that our past method of praying evolves into a form of meditation, whether or not we think we know how to meditate. Praying only for God's will and for the power to carry that out redirects our personal and worldly fixations and allows us to concentrate only on the will of our Higher Power. It empties our minds of our preoccupation with ourselves, making it possible to experience God's presence.

If we place our will in God's care, and pray sincerely for guidance, we find ourselves trusting that our will is being redirected. We then experience the courage and power to act according to God's will for us. Seeking higher guidance is an experience in humility, because we are so accustomed to running our lives by our own plan and making demands on God to give us what we think we want. Our own desires and opinions are so much a part of us that we may, at times, view the will of a Higher Power as a manifestation of what we think should happen.

We use prayer and meditation to improve our conscious contact with God as we understand God. As we work Step Eleven, we may see signs of progress, such as a deep sense of gratitude accompanied by a feeling of actually "belonging" in the world at last. We also may feel more secure as we develop a sense of being guided and sustained while we proceed with our activities. If we understand and follow the Program carefully, some of the changes in our lives will appear miraculous; others will be more gradual as we gain the skills we need to sustain our recovery.

GUIDELINES FOR PRAYER AND MEDITATION

An overview of prayer and meditation for a given day may be outlined as follows:

At the beginning of the day, review your priorities and:

- Ask your Higher Power for direction in your thoughts and actions.
  - To keep you aware of self-pity, dishonesty or excessive self-interest.
  - To provide the guidance needed to take care of any problems.
- Ask your Higher Power for freedom from self-will.

During the day, in moments of indecision or fear:

- Ask your Higher Power for inspiration and guidance.
- Reflect on Step Three and turn it over.
  - Relax and breathe deeply several times.
  - Be aware of any desire to "be right."
- Pray to your Higher Power as often as necessary during the day.
  - "Higher Power, please help me remove this _____" (feeling, obsession, addiction, etc.).
- If possible, call a support person to identify and share what is happening.

At the end of the day, review the events that happened and:

- Reflect on Step Ten and take a personal inventory.
  - Ask your Higher Power for guidance in taking corrective action where necessary.
- Ask for knowledge of your Higher Power's will for you.
- Forgive yourself and ask your Higher Power to help you learn from your errors. This review is not intended to cause obsessive thinking, worry, remorse or morbid reflection.
- Give thanks to your Higher Power for the guidance and blessings that were part of the day.

JUST FOR TODAY

I will take a good look at myself and see that I have many addictive and compulsive traits that have become dominant in my life. I am at the mercy of these traits and unable to manage them. Seeing this, I admit that I need help.

I will acknowledge the presence of a Power greater than myself who has created me, is aware of all my needs and is fully capable of healing me and restoring me to a condition of clarity and stability. This power is God as I choose to understand God.

I will let go of the inclination to figure out my problems with my mind. No more analyzing…no more questioning. I now make a conscious decision to turn my life and my will over to the care and keeping of God. I surrender the thinking that tells me I must "run my own show" and make my own life happen. I am ready to be a transformed (changed) person, beginning now.

I will release the past, letting go of my guilt or regrets about what happened "back then." Finding fault or blaming myself and/or others keeps me stuck in the past.

I will forgive myself and others for the way we've been. I realize that our actions have arisen out of fear and insecurity. I now allow myself and others to "be." I no longer pass judgment on our lives, our chosen paths or our patterns of growth.

I will drop all anxiety about the future. I will live **this day** with as much joy, trust and serenity as I can, realizing that this day is all I can handle.

I will let go of my tendencies to be dependent on persons, possessions and patterns to fulfill me. I recognize that these things are only a temporary part of my existence and cannot provide the lasting security, inner peace or true freedom that I yearn to experience on a daily basis.

I will take responsibility for all aspects of my life: my choices, my feelings, my physical and mental health, my spiritual well-being, my paths of growth and the principles and values by which I live.

I will utilize all the energies within me that contribute to the betterment of my life and to the lives of others (e.g., expressing honesty, integrity and kindness). To all else, I firmly say, "No, thank you."

I will thank God for the opportunity to be set free from old attitudes and behavior patterns that prevent me from moving in the direction of my needed healing.

I will willingly share with others the wisdom, peace and strength I have received through this Program.

I will go forth into this day with enthusiasm, believing in my own value and worthiness, and with the determination to enjoy this day and give it my positive best, come what may.

What Is Best

O Lord, you know what is best for me. Let this or that be done, as you please. Give what you will, how much you will, and when you will.

(Taken from *12 Step Prayers for A Way Out*, page 85)

STEP TWELVE

Having had a spiritual awakening as the result of these steps, we tried to carry this message to others and to practice these principles in all our affairs.

The Twelfth Step is the goal we were seeking when we began our journey toward healing and recovery. As we worked our way through the Steps, personal intuition told us that there was hope for us when we completed the cycle of this process. No mystery surrounds the Twelve Steps when we realize that they really work for those who are willing to risk self-discovery through surrender to a Higher Power. If we have practiced the other eleven Steps to the best of our ability, we will receive all of the gifts that result from our surrendering to a Higher Power and can pass them on to others.

The process of working the Steps can be compared to the transformation of a caterpillar into a butterfly. The caterpillar does not understand that it will become a butterfly. All parts of the death of its former identity and its rebirth in the cocoon must be experienced to bring about the transformation. The story is told of a man who noticed a cocoon attached to a branch of a bush in his yard. As he started to pull it from the bush and throw it away, he noticed the end opening and a butterfly struggling to escape. In an effort to help the emerging butterfly, he carefully cut the cocoon apart. The butterfly feebly crawled from the opened cocoon and, within a few hours, died. It needed the strength it would have gained from its struggle for freedom to survive in the outside world. Similarly, our working the Steps is a process we must complete by ourselves. Any attempt by another person to do our work or find our answers for us would limit our ability to gain the emotional strength we need to function in a healthy manner.

If we use the awakening of our new state of consciousness and being, our spiritual relationship with God can be a gift. It is usually accompanied by a shift in our value system—where there was darkness, we now see light. For most of us, our awakening is subtle and can best be appreciated in hindsight. The maturity we gain by working the Steps enables us to view many past experiences, especially painful ones, as spiritual in nature. Our spiritual growth, therefore, can be viewed as the sum of these individual experiences. With each, we can identify the ways in which our Higher Power has guided us.

We become increasingly able to feel, do and believe what would not be possible had we relied solely on our own resources. We find that we possess honesty, humility, peace of mind and love to a degree we had never imagined. New values, based on an understanding of ourselves as children of God, give emotional and spiritual balance to our lives. With the help of our Higher Power, we continually discover new qualities and abilities in ourselves, as well as in those around us.

Spiritual growth is an ongoing process—it may have begun early in the Steps, but it will continue for the rest of our lives. Spiritual growth is not a distinct event with a clear beginning and ending; it is a continuing evolution of becoming more compassionate, loving, caring and content. Our relationships with our families improve as we draw closer, yet we recognize each other's need for independence. We rarely have unrealistic expectations of ourselves, and we accept others as they are, not as we might want them to be.

Because we know this Program works, and it is working for us, we are ready to share it with others. The message we carry to those who are in bondage, as we once were, is a liberating one. Sharing the message strengthens our own recovery and advances our spiritual growth. In return, the new strengths and insights we receive help us continue our growth in heart, mind and spirit. Our ability to effect change convinces others of the value of the Steps and, in this way, the Program grows and prospers.

There is no specific way to "carry this message to others" besides telling our stories as honestly as we can—by explaining what our lives were like, what happened to us as a result of the Steps and how our lives have changed. This is one time when truly being ourselves is the gift we give to others. It can happen anywhere—when we are called upon to do volunteer work, share in meetings, interact with co-workers and family members. Sharing our story with others often helps them recognize their own needs and teaches us more about humility and honesty. As we share our experience, strength and hope with newcomers, we can inspire them to solve their own problems, look at themselves honestly and stop blaming others for their pain.

Working with newcomers can be extremely rewarding, as it gives us a heightened appreciation of how far we have come, thanks to the Program. As we reflect on where we were when first introduced to the Program, we are filled with empathy for those who come to the Program feeling troubled, confused, resentful and seeking "instant relief." As they get to know us, they will descover that the decision to join is an individual one, made by most of us when we decided we had hurt and suffered enough and were willing to surrender.

Carrying the message to others may mean:

- Offering guidance and help to newcomers as they learn that the Program can be successful only through a commitment to do the work.

- Encouraging newcomers to be patient and gentle with themselves while working the Program one day at a time.

- Acknowledging to newcomers that revelations from working the Steps may be both painful and rewarding.

A recurring message throughout the Twelve Steps is the importance of humility and surrender to our Higher Power. As we *"practice these principles in all our affairs,"* the key factor in this process is our relationship with our Higher Power. Working closely with our Higher Power keeps us on the right course and helps us maintain our inner peace—a state we cannot achieve independently. It can only come to us when we admit powerlessness and are willing to work on our spiritual development, one day at a time.

Sometimes we become discouraged and lose sight of our progress. If this happens, we can compare our past behavior to our present and ask ourselves:

- Are we less isolated and no longer afraid of people in authority?

- Have we stopped seeking approval from others and accepted ourselves as we really are?

- Are we more selective in choosing those with whom we develop relationships, and more able to keep our own identity intact while in a relationship?

- Have we developed the ability to express our feelings?

- Have we stopped trying to dominate others?

- Are we no longer behaving childishly by turning friends or spouses into protective parents, or by being overly dependent?

- Are we paying attention to the needs of our inner child?

Affirmative answers indicate the extent of our progress toward a healthier and better way of living.

As we practice our new behaviors in our daily affairs, life in general seems to be working better. For some of us, the new behaviors we use in family and work environments have a profoundly positive effect, and we see our loved ones embarking on the road to recovery in their own lives. This is truly a manifestation of our cooperation with our Higher Power. We can now see how the changes in our lives and our behavior can impact the lives of others.

A key to practicing the Program in all our affairs is using the Steps as an integral part of our lives. The discipline of taking a problem through all the Steps need not be a time-consuming process. Most of our confusion will we eliminated if we invite the unfailing support and guidance from our Higher Power. The end result leaves us with a sense of inner peace and increases our confidence in our ability to deal directly with each of our problems at any time.

The most confounding, yet the simplest, truth is that the Program is useful for *all* areas of our lives. All we need to do "in all our affairs" is to be willing to work the Steps and then "let go." The process is gradual, regenerative and never-ending. We slowly become more responsive to our Higher Power, and thus learn the meaning of love, growth, peace and serenity.

Please, Lord

Please, Lord, teach us to laugh again; but God, don't ever let us forget that we cried.

(Taken from *12 Step Prayers for A Way Out,* page 95)

TWELVE STEP REVIEW

Identify a situation or condition in your life that is currently a source of resentment, fear, sadness, or anger. It may involve relationships (family, work, or personal), work environment, health or self-esteem. Describe the situation and indicate why it is a concern.

Use the following questions to apply the principles of the Twelve Steps to the above.

Step One: In what ways are you powerless over this situation or condition, and how is it showing you the unmanageability of your life?

Step Two: How do you see your Higher Power as assisting you in being restored to wholeness?

Step Three: How does being willing to turn your life over to the care of God assist you in dealing with this?

Step Four: What character traits have surfaced (e.g., fear of abandonment or authority figures, control, approval seeking, obsessive/compulsive behavior, rescuing, taking inappropriate responsibility, not expressing feelings)?

Step Five: Admit your wrongs to God, to yourself and to another human being.

Step Six: Are you entirely ready to work in partnership with God to remove your ineffective behaviors? If not, explain.

Step Seven: Can you humbly ask God for help in removing your shortcomings? If not, what stands in your way?

Step Eight: Make a list of the persons harmed.

Step Nine: What amends are necessary, and how will you make them?

Step Ten: Review the above Steps to be sure that nothing has been overlooked.

Step Eleven: Take a moment for prayer or meditation, asking for knowledge of God's will for you. What did you discover?

Step Twelve: How can your understanding and spiritual guidance assist you in dealing with this problem?

APPENDIX ONE

SELF-HELP RESOURCES

Adult Children of Alcoholics
Central Service Board
P.O. Box 3216
Torrance, California 90505
(213) 534-1815

Al-Anon/Alateen
Family Group
 Headquarters, Inc.
Madison Square Station
New York, New York 10010
(212) 683-1771

Alcoholics Anonymous
World Services, Inc.
468 Park Avenue
New York, New York 10016
(212) 686-1100

Co-Dependents Anonymous
P.O. Box 33577
Phoenix, Arizona
 85067-3577
(602) 944-0141

Debtors Anonymous
P.O. Box 20322
New York, New York
 10025-9992

Emotions Anonymous
P.O. Box 4245
St. Paul, Minnesota 55104

Gamblers Anonymous
P.O. Box 17173
Los Angeles, California
 90017

Narcotics Anonymous
World Service Office
16155 Wyandotte Street
Van Nuys, California 91406
(818) 780-3951

National Association for
 Children of Alcoholics
31706 Coast Highway,
 Suite 201
South Laguna, California
 92677
(714) 499-3889

National Council on
 Alcoholism
12 West 21st Street
New York, New York 10010
(212) 206-6770

Overeaters Anonymous
World Service Office
2190 190th Street
Torrance, California 90504
(213) 320-7941

Sexaholics Anonymous
P.O. Box 300
Simi Valley, California 93062
(805) 581-3343

STEP-STUDY WRITING
WORKSHOP OVERVIEW

Following is an outline of what to expect from participating in a Step-Study Writing Workshop using the book *The 12 Steps—A Way Out* ($14.95).

- During the first three weeks, the meeting remains open so that anyone interested in experiencing the meeting format is welcomed to do so. This is the first such meeting.

- After the third week, small family groups are formed. These groups are an important part of the Step-Study process and encourage the development of trusting, supportive relationships during the weeks that follow.

- Beginning with the fourth week, the meeting is facilitated by each family group on a rotating basis. The meeting format is in Appendix Two of the workbook.

- Two weeks are devoted to completing most of the Steps.

- Read the workbook material and complete as much of the writing as possible in a timely manner.

- The writing exercise for each Step (Appendix Three), is the focus of the weekly meeting. Time is spent at the beginning of the meeting to complete the exercise, which then becomes the basis for family sharing.

- Remember that you are doing this work for your own personal growth. Set your own pace and accept your progress without having unrealistic expectations of yourself.

- This Program is worked most successfully one day at a time.

APPENDIX THREE

SUGGESTED READING

Alcoholics Anonymous. **The Big Book.** New York, NY: Alcoholics Anonymous World Services, Inc.

Alcoholics Anonymous. **Twelve Steps—Twelve Traditions.** New York, NY: Alcoholics Anonymous World Services, Inc.

Beattie, Melody. **Codependent No More.** New York, NY: Harper and Row Publishers, Inc.

Black, Claudia. **It Will Never Happen To Me.** New York, NY: Ballantine Books.

Bradshaw, John. **Bradshaw on: The Family.** Deerfield Beach, FL: Health Communications, Inc.

Covington, Stephanie & Beckett, Liana. **Leaving The Enchanted Forest: The Path From Relationship Addiction To Intimacy.** New York, NY: Harper & Row.

Fishel, Ruth. **The Journey Within—A Spiritual Path To Recovery.** Deerfield Beach, FL: Health Communications, Inc.

Friel, John and Friel, Linda. **Adult Children—The Secrets of Dysfunctional Families.** Deerfield Beach, FL: Health Communications, Inc.

Friends in Recovery. **The 12 Steps—A Way Out.** San Diego, CA: Recovery Publications.

Friends in Recovery. **The Twelve Steps—A Spiritual Journey.** San Diego, CA: Recovery Publications.

Friends in Recovery. **The Twelve Steps for Christians.** San Diego, CA: Recovery Publications.

Kritsberg, Wayne. **The Adult Children of Alcoholics Syndrome.** Deerfield Beach, FL: Health Communications, Inc.

Larson, Earnie and Hegarty, Carol. **Days of Healing— Days of Joy.** New York, NY: Harper/Hazelden.

Lasater, Lane. **Recovery From Compulsive Behavior.** Deerfield Beach, FL: Health Communications, Inc.

Lerner, Rokelle. **Daily Affirmations—For Adult Children of Alcoholics.** Deerfield Beach, FL: Health Communications, Inc.

Pollard, Dr. John K., III. **Self Parenting: Your Complete Guide to Inner Conversations.** Malibu, CA: Generic Human Studies Publishing.

Ross, Ron **When I Grow Up... I Want To Be An Adult.** San Diego, CA: Recovery Publications.

Wegscheider-Cruse, Sharon. **Learning To Love Yourself.** Deerfield Beach, FL: Health Communications, Inc.

Whitfield, Charles. **Healing the Child Within.** Deerfield Beach, FL: Health Communications, Inc.

Woititz, Janet. **Adult Children of Alcoholics.** Deerfield Beach, FL: Health Communications, Inc.

Woititz, Janet G. **Struggle For Intimacy.** Deerfield Beach, FL: Health Communications, Inc.